FAMOUS ITALIAN OPERA ARIAS

A Dual-Language Book

EDITED AND TRANSLATED BY

ELLEN H. BLEILER

DOVER PUBLICATIONS, INC.

Mineola, New York

Copyright

Copyright © 1996 by Dover Publications, Inc.
All rights reserved under Pan American and International Copyright Conventions.

Bibliographical Note

Famous Italian Opera Arias: A Dual-Language Book is a new work, first published by Dover Publications, Inc., in 1996. The Italian texts are reprinted from standard sources. The English translations and all other elements of the book are new, specially prepared for the present edition.

Library of Congress Cataloging-in-Publication Data

Famous Italian opera arias : a dual-language book / edited and translated by Ellen H. Bleiler.
    p.   cm.
    Aria texts in Italian, reprinted from standard eds., with new English translation.
    Includes index.
    ISBN 0-486-29158-8 (pbk.)
    1. Operas—Excerpts—Librettos. I. Bleiler, Ellen H.
ML48.F3 1996   <Case>
782.1′026′8—dc20   95-41475
                                            CIP
                                          MN

Manufactured in the United States of America
Dover Publications, Inc., 31 East 2nd Street, Mineola, N.Y. 11501

Publisher's Note

Since opera is a universally loved and admired aspect of Italian culture, and cultural interests offer a matchless incentive to those learning a foreign language, it seemed natural to provide a dual-language anthology of major Italian opera arias. Included here are correct, reliable Italian texts and new literal line-for-line translations of 141 arias from 29 operas by 17 composers. The book is arranged alphabetically by composer; under each composer, the operas appear chronologically by year of first performance; under each opera, the arias appear in the order of the plot. An alphabetical index at the end of the volume allows ready access to each opera and aria. The headings in the text supply the birth and death years of the composers, the year in which each opera was first performed, the names and dates (where available) of the librettists, the names of the characters who sing the arias, and the act of the opera within which each aria falls.

The Italian texts, wherever possible, are given in the poetic form (regular meters, lines usually rhyming) originally supplied to the composer by the librettist. Where alternative versions of some lines exist, those ordinarily performed are adopted here. Brief immediate repetitions (of one or a few words) that were introduced by the composer (or brief added exclamations, such as "ah!") are not indicated in our text, but longer immediate repetitions, or repetitions of earlier words that occur later in the aria, are indicated by an "(etc.)" and the opening and closing words of the repetition. Where a composer purposely left out a couple of words which, in the original poem, completed the metrical or rhyme scheme, these words are included here within square brackets (examples in: Verdi, *Otello*, "Brindisi" and "Salce"). In instances where the composer remodeled the text drastically to suit his musical or dramatic purposes, only the final form given by the composer is printed here (extreme examples in: Puccini, *Tosca*, "Vissi d'arte"; *Madama Butterfly*, "Addio fiorito asil" and "Tu? tu? piccolo Iddio!").

Those who listen to entire operas, or to highlights recordings extracted from entire performances, are aware that in reality many "arias" that are presented as pure vocal solos in recital recordings involve the chorus or even other soloists. In the present volume such participation by others than the chief soloist is usually indicated merely by some such phrase (in square brackets) as "dialogue for Normanno, Raimondo and Chorus." On the other hand, the actual words of the other participants are given (in square brackets) when very brief, or when they are necessary to complete the meaning and/or the rhyme scheme of words assigned in the main "aria" to the chief soloist (very cogent examples: Bellini, *Norma*, "Casta diva"; Verdi, *Otello*, "Brindisi").*

The new English translations adhere as closely to the Italian text as differences in idiom and word order will allow. They claim to be more correct than most translations accompanying recordings, which frequently show symptoms of a lack of solid foundation in Italian grammar (confusion of parts of speech, nonrecognition of the subjunctive mode, etc.), a reliance on false cognates and a substitution of wild guesswork for conscientious dictionary searches, especially where the Italian vocabulary becomes recherché (as in texts by Boito). The almost cynical notion that Italian is such an easy language that it can be learned "by osmosis" invariably leads to the most ludicrous errors; the present volume wishes to strike a blow for accuracy. Some opera lovers may be surprised to learn the real meaning of certain phrases from their favorite arias.

When using this book to expand vocabulary and increase fluency in Italian, it is wise to be aware that, in common with most Italian poetry, these texts use special poetic forms and archaisms, and are not normally a source for phraseology in everyday conversation.

---

*Words that appear within parentheses (as, for example, in Bellini, *Norma*, "Casta diva") indicate stage "asides," words that are not meant to be heard by other characters onstage.

Contents

Vincenzo Bellini (1801–1835)

LA SONNAMBULA
(1831; libretto by Felice Romani, 1788–1865)

Ah! non credea mirarti (Amina, ACT II)

Ah! non credea mirarti
sì presto estinto, o fiore;
passasti al par d'amore
che un giorno solo durò.
[ELVINO: Io più non reggo
a tanto duolo.]
Potria novel vigore
il pianto mio donarti,
ma ravvivar l'amore
il pianto mio non può.

Ah! I had not thought to see you
withered so soon, o flower;
you disappeared quickly, like love,
that lasted only a day.
[ELVINO: I can no longer bear
so much sorrow.]
My tears might
give you fresh strength,
but my weeping can't
revive love.

Ah! Non giunge (Amina, ACT II)

Ah! Non giunge uman pensiero

al contento ond'io son piena:
a' miei sensi io credo appena;
tu m'affida, o mio tesor.
Ah, mi abbraccia, e sempre insieme,

sempre uniti in una speme,
della terra in cui viviamo

ci formiamo un ciel d'amor.

Ah! Human thought can't compre-
hend
the contentment that fills me:
I scarcely believe my senses;
give me assurance, o my treasure.
Ah, embrace me, and together
forever,
forever united in a single hope,
we'll shape the earth on which we
live
into a heaven of love.

NORMA *(1831; libretto by Felice Romani, 1788–1865)*

Casta diva (Norma, ACT I)

Io nei volumi arcani
leggo del cielo; in pagine di morte
della superba Roma è scritto il
　nome—
Ella un giorno morrà; ma non per
　voi.
Morrà pei vizi suoi,
qual consunta morrà. L'ora aspet-
　tate,
l'ora fatal che compia il gran
　decreto.
Pace v'intimo—e il sacro vischio io
　mieto.
Casta diva, che inargenti
queste sacre antiche piante,
a noi volgi il bel sembiante
senza nube e senza vel.
[OROVESO & CHORUS: Casta (etc.)
　. . . vel.]
Tempra tu de' cori ardenti,
tempra ancor lo zelo audace,
spargi in terra quella pace) (WITH
che regnar tu fai nel ciel.) CHORUS)

Fine al rito; e il sacro bosco

sia disgombro dai profani.
Quando il Nume irato e fosco
chiegga il sangue dei Romani,
dal Druïdico delubro
la mia voce tuonerà.
[CHORUS: Tuoni, e un sol del popol
　empio
non isfugga al giusto scempio,

e primier da noi percosso
il Proconsole cadrà.]
Sì, cadrà—punirlo io posso—

(Ma punirlo il cor non sa.)

I am reading the arcane volumes
of the sky; on pages of death
the name of haughty Rome is
　inscribed—
One day she will die; but not by
　your hands.
She will die of her own vices,
like a ravaged woman she will die.
　Await the hour,
the fatal hour that fulfills the
　grand decree.
I bid you peace—and I will pick the
　sacred mistletoe.
Chaste goddess who silvers
these sacred ancient trees,
turn your lovely face toward us,
cloudless and unveiled.
[OROVESO & CHORUS: Chaste (etc.)
　. . . unveiled.]
Continue to temper the bold zeal
of our ardent hearts,
spread over earth that peace)
which you cause to reign in } (WITH
　heaven.) CHORUS)

End the ritual; and let the sacred
　wood
be cleared of unholy ones.
When the wrathful and dark deity
demands the blood of the Romans,
my voice shall resound
from the Druids' temple.
[CHORUS: Let it resound, and of
　the impious nation
let not one escape his just
　slaughter,
and, the first to be struck by us,
the Proconsul shall fall.]
Yes, he will fall—I can chastise
　him—

(But my heart knows not how to
　chastise him.)

(Ah! Bello a me ritorna

del fido amor primiero;
e contro il mondo intero
difesa a te sarò.
Ah! Bello a me ritorna
del raggio tuo sereno;
e vita nel tuo seno,
e patria, e cielo avrò.)
[CHORUS: Sei lento, sì, sei lento,

o giorno di vendetta;
ma irato il Dio t'affretta

che il Tebro condannò.]
(Ah! riedi ancora
qual eri allora,
quando il cor ti diedi! etc.)

(Ah! Come back to me in the beauty
of your first true love;
and against the whole world
I shall be your protection.
Ah! Come back to me in the beauty
of your tranquil radiance;
and in your breast I'll find
life, homeland and heaven.)
[CHORUS: You are slow, yes, you are slow,
o day of vengeance;
but you are hastened by the angry god
who has condemned the Tiber.]
(Ah! return again
as you were then,
when I gave you my heart! etc.)

I PURITANI *(1835; libretto by Carlo Pepoli, 1796–1881)*

Son vergin vezzosa (Elvira, ACT I)

Son vergin vezzosa—in vesta di sposa,
son bianca ed umil—qual giglio d'April;
ho chiome odorose—cui cinser tue rose;
ho il seno gentil—del bel tuo monil.

I'm a comely maiden—in bridal dress,
I'm pale and modest—like an April lily;
my hair is fragrant—your roses encircle it;
my breast is ennobled—by your lovely necklace.

Qui la voce (Elvira, ACT II)

Qui la voce sua soave
mi chiamava—e poi sparì.

Qui giurava esser fedele,
poi crudele—ei mi fuggì!
Ah, mai più qui assorti insieme

nella gioia dei sospir?
Ah, rendetemi la speme
o lasciatemi morir!

Here his sweet voice
used to call me—and then disappeared.

Here he swore to be true,
then, cruel man—he shunned me!
Ah, never more absorbed together here
in the bliss of sighs?
Ah, restore my hope
or let me die!

Arrigo Boito (1842–1918)

MEFISTOFELE *(1868 & 1876; libretto by the composer)*

Dai campi, dai prati (Faust, ACT I)

Dai campi, dai prati che innonda	From the fields, from the meadows that the night
la notte, dai queti sentier	envelops, from the quiet footpaths
ritorno e di pace, di calma profonda	I return and am filled with peace,
son pieno, di sacro mister.	with profound calm, with sacred mystery.
Le torve passioni del core	My heart's grim passions
s'assonnano in placido obblio.	are drowsing off in tranquil forgetfulness.
Mi ferve soltanto l'amore	I am stirred only by love
dell'uomo! l'amore di Dio!	of mankind! love of God!
Dai campi, dai prati ritorno	I return from the fields, from the meadows,
e verso l'Evangel mi sento attratto,	and feel myself drawn to the Gospel,
m'accingo a meditar.	I shall get ready to meditate.

L'altra notte (Margherita, ACT III)

L'altra notte in fondo al mare	The other night, they threw
il mio bimbo hanno gittato,	my baby into the depths of the sea.
or per farmi delirare	Now, in order to drive me mad,
dicon ch'io l'abbia affogato.	they say that I have drowned him.
L'aura è fredda, il carcer fosco,	The air is cold, the prison dark,
e la mesta anima mia	and my mournful soul,
come il passero del bosco	like a woodland sparrow,
vola via. Ah! Pietà di me!	flies away. Ah! Have pity on me!
In letargico sopore	In a drowsy stupor
è mia madre addormentata,	my mother sleeps soundly
e per colmo dell'orrore	and, as the crowning horror,
dicon ch'io l'abbia attoscata.	they say I have poisoned her.
L'aura (etc.) . . . di me!	The air (etc.) . . . on me!

Alfredo Catalani (1854–1893)

LA WALLY (1892; libretto by Luigi Illica, 1857–1919)

Ebben? . . . Ne andrò lontana (Wally, ACT I)

Ebben? . . . Ne andrò lontana

come va l'eco della pia campana,
là, fra la neve bianca,
là, fra le nubi d'or
laddove la speranza
è rimpianto, è dolor!
O della madre mia casa gioconda,
la Wally andrà da te lontana assai,

e forse a te più non farà ritorno,

nè più la rivedrai!
Ne andrò (etc.) . . . d'or.
Ma fermo è il pie! Ne andiam!

Che lunga è la via!

Well then? . . . I'll go as far away
    from here
as the church bell's echo,
out there, amid the white snow,
out there, amid the golden clouds,
out there, where hope
is regret and sorrow!
O my mother's cheerful house,
Wally will go very far away from
    you,
and perhaps will never return to
    you,
and you'll not see her again!
I'll go away (etc.) . . . golden clouds.
But my feet are resolute! Let's be
    going!
What a long way it is!

Francesco Cilea (1866–1950)

ADRIANA LECOUVREUR
(1902; libretto by Arturo Colautti, 1851–1914)

Io son l'umile ancella (Adriana, ACT I)

Io son l'umile ancella
del Genio creator:
ei m'offre la favella,
io la diffondo ai cor . . .
Del verso io son l'accento,
l'eco del dramma uman,
il fragile strumento
vassallo della man . . .

I am the lowly handmaiden
of creative genius:
it presents me with speech,
I pour it into your hearts . . .
I am the sound of the verse,
the echo of the human drama,
the fragile instrument
that's servant to the hand . . .

Mite, gioconda, atroce,
Mi chiamo Fedeltà,
un soffio è la mia voce,
che al novo dì morrà.

Mild, merry, horrible,
my name is True Likeness,
my voice is a puff of air,
that will die as each new day
   dawns.

Poveri fiori (Adriana, ACT IV)

Poveri fiori,
gemme de' prati,
pur ieri nati,
oggi morenti,
quai giuramenti
d'infido cor!
L'ultimo bacio,
o il bacio primo,
ecco v'imprimo,
soave e forte
bacio di morte,
bacio d'amor . . . .
Tutto è finito!
Col vostro olezzo
muoia il disprezzo:
Con voi d'un giorno
senza ritorno
cessi l'error!
Tutto è finito!

Poor flowers,
jewels of the meadows,
born just yesterday,
dying today,
like the vows
of a faithless heart!
The last kiss,
or the first kiss,
I imprint it on you here,
mild and powerful
kiss of death,
kiss of love . . . .
Everything is over!
Let scorn die
along with your fragrance:
Along with you
let the delusion of a day
that cannot return end!
Everything is over!

Gaetano Donizetti (1797–1848)

L'ELISIR D'AMORE

(1832; libretto by Felice Romani, 1788–1865)

Udite, udite, o rustici! (Dulcamara, ACT I)

Udite, udite, o rustici!
Attenti, non fiatate.
Io già suppongo e immagino
che al par di me sappiate
ch'io sono quel gran medico,
dottore enciclopedico,

Listen, listen, o countryfolk!
Pay attention, don't breathe a word.
I already suppose and believe
that, like me, you know
that I am that great doctor,
comprehensive physician,

chiamato Dulcamara,
la cui vertù preclara,
e i portenti infiniti
son noti all'universo
e . . . e . . . e in altri siti.
Benefattor degl'uomini,
riparator de' mali,
in pochi giorni io sgombero,
io spazzo gli spedali,
e la salute a vendere
per tutto il mondo io vo.
Compratela, compratela,
per poco io ve la do.
È questo l'odontalgico
mirabile liquore,
dei topi e delle cimici
possente distruttore,
i cui certificati
autentici, bollati,
toccar vedere e leggere
a ciaschedun farò.
Per questo mio specifico,

simpatico, prolifico,
un uom settuagenario
e valetudinario,
nonno di dieci bamboli
ancora diventò.
Per questo "tocca e sana"
in breve settimana
più d'un afflitta vedova
di piangere cessò.
O voi matrone rigide,
ringiovanir bramate?
Le vostre rughe incomode

con esso cancellate.
Volete voi donzelle
ben liscia aver la pelle?
Voi giovani galanti
per sempre avere amanti?
Comprate il mio specifico,
per poco ve lo do.
Da bravi giovinotti,
da brave vedovette,

called Dulcamara,
whose extraordinary power
and boundless wonders
are known to the entire world
and . . . and . . . and elsewhere.
Benefactor of mankind,
curer of diseases,
in a few days I empty out,
I clear out the hospitals,
and to sell good health
I travel all over the world.
Buy it, buy it!
I'll give it to you for a low price!
This is that miraculous liquid
which cures toothache,
powerful destroyer
of rats and bedbugs,
whose authentic, stamped
certificates
I'll allow each one of you
to touch, to see and read.
By means of this agreeable, pro-
    ductive
remedy of mine,
a septuagenarian
and valetudinarian
still became grandfather
of ten babies.
By means of this instant cure
in the short space of a week
more than one distressed widow
stopped weeping.
O you proper matrons,
do you yearn to be rejuvenated?
Be rid of your troublesome
    wrinkles
with this.
You damsels, do you want
to have glossy skin?
You young swains,
always to have lovers?
Buy my remedy,
I'll give it to you for a low price.
As gallant young men,
as fine little widows,

comprate il mio specifico,
per poco ve lo do.
Ei move i paralitici,
spedisce gli apopletici,
gli asmatici, gli asfitici,
gl'isterici, i diabetici;
guarisce timpanitidi,
e scrofole e rachitidi,
persin il mal di fegato
che in moda diventò.
Comprate il mio specifico,
per poco ve lo do.
Avanti, avanti, vedove,

avanti, avanti, bamboli.

L'ho portato per la posta,
da lontano mille miglia.
Mi direte: Quanto costa?

Quanto vale la bottiglia?
Cento scudi? No. Trenta? No.
  Venti?
Nessuno si sgomenti,
per provarvi il mio contento
di sì amico accoglimento,
io vi voglio, o buona gente,
uno scudo regalar.
[CHORUS: Uno scudo? Veramente?
Più brav'uom non si può dar.]
Ecco qua: così stupendo,
sì balsamico elisire,
tutta Europa sa ch'io vendo
niente men di nove lire:
ma siccome è pur palese,
ch'io son nato nel paese,
per tre lire a voi lo cedo;
sol tre lire a voi richiedo.
(Gaetano, tromba!)
Così chiaro è come il sole,
che a ciascuno che lo vuole,
uno scudo bello e netto
in saccoccia io faccio entrar.
Ah! di patria il caldo
    affetto   } (WITH
gran miracoli può far. } CHORUS)

buy my remedy,
I'll give it to you for a low price.
It makes paralytics move,
cures apoplectics,
asthmatics, those short of breath,
hysterics, diabetics;
it cures earaches,
and scrofula and rickets,
and even the liver trouble
that's become fashionable.
Buy my remedy,
I'll give it to you for a low price.
Come forward, come forward,
    widows,
come forward, come forward,
    kiddies.
I've carried it by stagecoach
from a thousand miles away.
You say to me: "How much does it
    cost?
How much is a bottle worth?
A hundred scudi?" No. "Thirty?"
    No. "Twenty?"
No one need worry,
in order to show my pleasure
at such a friendly welcome,
I want, o good folk,
to make you a gift of one scudo.
[CHORUS: One scudo? Really?
There can't be a finer fellow.]
Here it is! so stupendous,
so soothing an elixir,
all Europe knows that I sell it
for no less than nine lire;
but since it's well known
that I was born in this region,
I'll let you have it for three lire;
I ask only three lire of you.
(Gaetano, the trumpet!)
It's as plain as the sun
that I'll slip a pretty scudo
neatly into the pocket
of anyone who wants it.
Ah! warm love for one's
    homeland   } (WITH
can cause great miracles. } CHORUS)

Una furtiva lagrima (Nemorino, ACT II)

Una furtiva lagrima	A secret tear
negl'occhi suoi spuntò;	sprang from her eye;
quelle festose giovani	she seemed to envy
invidiar sembrò.	those merry young women.
Che più cercando io vo?	What more do I seek?
M'ama, sì, m'ama, lo vedo.	She loves me, yes, she loves me, I see it.
Un solo istante i palpiti	Only for an instant to feel
del suo bel cor sentir!	her sweet heart beating!
I miei sospir confondere	For a little while to mingle my sighs
per poco a' suoi sospir!	with her sighs!
Cielo, si può morir;	Heavens, a man can die;
di più non chiedo,	I ask for nothing more,
si può morir d'amor.	a man can die of love.

LUCREZIA BORGIA

(1833; libretto by Felice Romani, 1788–1865)

Brindisi: Il segreto per esser felici (Orsini, ACT II)

Il segreto per esser felici	The secret of being happy
so per prova e l'insegno agli amici:	I know from experience and I teach it to my friends:
Sia sereno, sia nubilo il cielo,	Let the sky be fair or cloudy,
ogni tempo sia caldo, sia gelo,	let it be hot or cold any time,
scherzo e bevo, e derido gl'insani	I joke and drink, and laugh at the madmen
che si dan del futuro pensier.	who worry about the future.
Non curiamo l'incerto domani,	Let's not care about tomorrow's uncertainties
se quest'oggi n'è dato goder.	if we can enjoy today.
[additional dialogue between stanzas]	[additional dialogue between stanzas]
Profittiamo degl'anni fiorenti,	Let's take advantage of our blossoming years,
il piacer li fa correr più lenti;	pleasure makes them go by more slowly;
se vecchiezza con livida faccia	if old age with its livid face
stammi a tergo e mia vita minaccia,	stands behind me and threatens my life,
scherzo e bevo, e derido gl'insani	I joke and drink, and laugh at the madmen
che si dan del futuro pensier.	who worry about the future.
Non curiamo l'incerto domani (etc.).	Let's not care about tomorrow's uncertainties (etc.).

LUCIA DI LAMMERMOOR

(1835; libretto by Salvatore Cammarano, 1801–1852)

Il dolce suono (Lucia, ACT II)

Il dolce suono
mi colpì di sua voce! Ah! quella
    voce
m'è qui nel cor discesa!
Edgardo! io ti son resa,
Edgardo! ah! Edgardo mio!
sì, ti son resa;
fuggita io son da' tuoi nemici.
Un gelo mi serpeggia nel sen!
Trema ogni fibra! Vacilla il piè!
Presso la fonte meco t'assidi
    alquanto,
sì, presso la fonte meco t'assidi!
Ohimè! sorge il tremendo fantasma
e ne separa!
Ahimè, ahimè, Edgardo!
Edgardo! ah! il fantasma ne separa!

Qui ricovriamo, Edgardo,
a piè dell'ara.
Sparsa è di rose! Un'armonia
    celeste,
di', non ascolti? Ah! l'inno

suona di nozze! Ah, l'inno di nozze!
Il rito per noi s'appresta. Oh me
    felice!
Oh gioia che si sente, e non si dice!

Ardon gl'incensi—Splendon
le sacre faci intorno!
Ecco il ministro! Porgimi
la destra! Oh lieto giorno! oh lieto!

Alfin son tua, alfin sei mio,

a me ti dona un Dio.
[dialogue for Normanno, Raimon-
    do and Chorus]

The sweet sound
of his voice has struck me! Ah!
    that voice
has entered my heart here!
Edgardo! I'm restored to you,
Edgardo, ah! my Edgardo!
Yes, I'm restored to you;
I've escaped from your enemies.
A chill crawls through my breast!
Every nerve quivers! My feet totter!
Sit with me by the fountain for a
    while,
yes, sit with me by the fountain!
Alas! the fearful ghost rises up
and separates us!
Alas! Alas! Edgardo!
Edgardo! Ah! The ghost separates
    us!
Let's seek refuge here, Edgardo,
at the foot of the altar.
It's strewn with roses! Tell me,
    don't you hear
heavenly music? Ah! The wedding
    hymn
sounds! Ah, the wedding hymn!
They're preparing the ceremony
    for us! Oh, how happy I am!
Oh! joy that is felt and can't be
    expressed!
The incense burns! The holy lights
shine all around!
Here is the pastor! Give me
your right hand! Oh joyous day!
    oh joyous!
At last I'm yours, at last you're
    mine,
God bestows you on me.
[dialogue for Normanno, Raimon-
    do and Chorus]

Ogni piacer più grato,
sì, ogni piacere mi fia con te
diviso,—
Del ciel clemente un riso
la vita a noi sarà.
[dialogue for Raimondo, Enrico
and Chorus]
Che chiedi?
Ah, me misera!
Non mi guardar sì fiero,
segnai quel foglio, è vero, sì, è vero.

Nell'ira sua terribile
calpesta, oh Dio, l'anello!
Mi maledice! Ah! vittima
fui d'un crudel fratello:
ma ognor, ognor t'amai,
ognor, Edgardo,
sì, ognor, ognor t'amai
[dialogue for Enrico and Raimondo]
ah! e t'amo ancor!
Edgardo mio, sì, te lo giuro!
Ognor (etc.).
Chi mi nomasti? Arturo!

Tu nomasti, Arturo!
Ah! non fuggir! Ah, per pietà!—

No, non fuggir! ah perdon!

[dialogue for Enrico, Raimondo
and Chorus]
Ah! no, non fuggir, Edgardo!
Spargi d'amaro pianto
il mio terrestre velo,
mentre lassù nel cielo,
io pregherò per te.
Al giunger tuo soltanto
fia bello il ciel per me!
[dialogue for Enrico, Raimondo
and Chorus]
Spargi (etc.) . . . per me!
Ah! ch'io spiri accanto a te,
appresso a te!

All the greatest delights,
yes, all delights I shall share with
you,—
our life will be
a smile from merciful heaven.
[dialogue for Raimondo, Enrico
and Chorus]
What do you want?
Ah! Wretched me!
Don't look at me so fiercely,
I signed that paper, it's true, yes,
it's true.

In his awful rage
he stamps on the ring, oh God!
He curses me! Ah! I was the victim
of a cruel brother:
but I always, always loved you,
always, Edgardo,
yes, I always, always loved you
[dialogue for Enrico and Raimondo]
ah! and I love you still!
Yes, my Edgardo, I swear it to you!
I always (etc.).
Whom did you speak to me of?
Arturo!
You spoke of Arturo!
Ah! Don't run away! Ah, for pity's
sake—

No, don't run away! Ah forgive
me!

[dialogue for Enrico, Raimondo
and Chorus]
Ah! No, don't run away, Edgardo!
Shed bitter tears
on my earthly shroud,
while up there in heaven
I'll pray for you.
Only when you arrive
will heaven be beautiful for me!
[dialogue for Enrico, Raimondo
and Chorus]
Shed (etc.) . . . for me!
Ah! That I might die beside you,
close to you!

Fra poco a me ricovero (Edgardo, Act III)

Tomba degli avi miei, l'ultimo avanzo d'una stirpe infelice,	Tomb of my ancestors, ah, receive the last remnant of an unfortunate lineage.
deh! raccogliete voi. Cessò dell'ira il breve foco . . . sul nemico acciaro	The brief flame of anger has ceased . . . I shall abandon myself
abbandonarmi vo'. Per me la vita è orrendo peso! l'universo intero	to my enemy's steel. For me life is a fearful burden! the whole universe
è un deserto per me senza Lucia! Di faci tuttavia splende il castello . . . Ah! scarsa fu la notte al tripudio! Ingrata donna!	is a desert to me without Lucia! The castle still blazes with lights . . . Ah! The night was too brief for their merriment! Ungrateful woman!
Mentr'io mi struggo in disperato pianto, tu ridi, esulti accanto al felice consorte!	While I languish in hopeless weeping, you laugh and exult at the side of your happy husband!
Tu delle gioie in seno, io della morte!	You in the bosom of joy, I in death's!
Fra poco a me ricovero darà negletto avello, una pietosa lagrima non scenderà su quello!	Soon an untended grave will give me shelter; no pitying tear will fall on it!
Ah! fin degli estinti, ahi misero! manca il conforto a me.	Ah! even the comforts of the dead are denied to me, unhappy man!
Tu pur, tu pur dimentica quel marmo dispregiato: mai non passarvi, o barbara, del tuo consorte a lato.	You, even you, please forget this despised tombstone: never pass by here, cruel woman, at your husband's side.
Rispetta almen le ceneri di chi morìa per te!	At least respect the dust of him who died for you!
Mai non passarvi, tu lo dimentica, rispetta almeno chi muore per te!	Never pass by here, forget this place, at least respect him who dies for you!

Tu che a Dio (Edgardo, Act III)

Tu che a Dio spiegasti l'ali, o bell'alma innamorata, ti rivolgi a me placata,	You that have taken wing to God, o beautiful, beloved soul, look back, pacified, at me,

teco ascenda il tuo fedel.	let your faithful one ascend with you.

Ah! se l'ira dei mortali	Ah! If the wrath of humans
fece a noi sì cruda guerra,	waged so cruel a battle against us,
se divisi fummo in terra,	if we were parted on earth,
ne congiunga il Nume in ciel.	let God unite us in heaven.
O bell'alma innamorata!	O beautiful, beloved soul!
Ne congiunga il Nume in ciel (etc.).	Let God unite us in heaven (etc.).
Io ti seguo—	I am following you—
Morir voglio.	I wish to die.
A te vengo—o bell'alma,— ti rivolgi, ah! al tuo fedel. } (WITH RAIMONDO & CHORUS)	I'm coming to you— o beautiful soul— look back at me, ah! at your faithful one. } (WITH RAIMONDO & CHORUS)

LA FIGLIA DEL REGGIMENTO

(La Fille du Régiment; 1840; original French libretto by Jules-Henri Vernoy de Saint-Georges, 1799–1875, and Jean-François-Alfred Bayard, 1796–1853; Italian translation by Calisto Bassi [dates unavailable])

Lo dice ognuno (Maria, ACT I)

Lo dice ognuno . . . ciascun lo sa,	They all say so, everyone knows,
è il Reggimento ch'egual non ha,	it's the regiment that has no peer,
il solo a cui credenza fa	the only one with credit
ogni taverna della città;	at every tavern in town;
il Reggimento che ovunque andò	the regiment that has dampened the spirits
mariti e amanti disanimò.	of husbands and lovers wherever it has gone.
Ma ben supremo della beltà!	Oh, supreme gift of good looks!
Egli è là, davver, proprio là,	Here it is, indeed, it's right here,
quell'undicesimo ch'egual non ha.	that Eleventh that has no peer.
[lines for Tonio, Sulpizio and Chorus]	[lines for Tonio, Sulpizio and Chorus]
Tante battaglie ei guadagnò	So many battles has it won
che il nostro Augusto già decretò	that our prince has already decreed
ch'ogni soldato (se scampo avrà)	that he will appoint each soldier (if he survives)
gran Maresciallo nominerà.	a Grand Marshal.
Perchè gli è questo il Reggimento	Because for him this is the regiment

più vincitore, più bello attento

che un sesso teme, che l'altro
    adora . . .
Egli è là (etc.) . . . non ha.

that's most victorious, handsome
    and diligent,
which one sex fears and the other
    adores . . .
Here it is (etc.) . . . no peer.

Amici miei (Tonio, ACT I)

Amici miei, che allegro giorno!
Le vostre insegne io seguirò.
Sol per amore a voi ritorno,

e un grande eroe diventerò.
Ah sì! Colei ond'io sospiro
ebbe pietade del mio martiro,
e questa speme desiata ognor
altera i sensi ed il mio cor.
Amici miei (etc.) [leading to con-
    certed number with Chorus]

My friends, what a happy day!
I'll follow your banners.
Only out of love do I come back to
    you,
and I'll become a great hero.
Ah, yes! The one for whom I sigh
had pity on my suffering,
and this ever longed-for wish
affects my senses and my heart.
My friends (etc.) [leading to con-
    certed number with Chorus]

LA FAVORITA

(La Favorite; 1840; original French libretto by Alphonse Royer, 1803–1875, and Gustave Vaëz, 1812–1862; Italian translation by Calisto Bassi [dates unavailable])

Vien, Leonora (King [Alfonso XI of Castille], ACT II)

Vien, Leonora, a' piedi tuoi
serto e soglio il cor ti dona.
Ah! se amare il re tu puoi,
mai del dono si pentirà!
Chè per soglio e per corona
gli riman la tua beltà!
Ah! mia Leonora, deh! vieni a me.
De' nemici tuoi lo sdegno
disfidar saprò per te.
Se ti cessi e l'alma e il regno,

io per gli altri ancor son re.
De' miei dì compagna io voglio

farti, o bella, innanzi al ciel;

Come, Leonora, my heart places
coronet and throne at your feet.
Ah, if you can love the king
he will never repent of his gifts!
For your beauty remains to him
in place of throne and crown!
Ah! my Leonora, do come to me.
For your sake I can defy
your enemies' anger.
If I have ceded to you both my soul
    and my kingdom,
I am still king to the others.
In heaven's presence, o beauteous
    one,
I wish to make you the sharer of
    my life;

al mio fianco unita in soglio,

al mio fianco nell'avel.

at my side, joined with me on the throne,

at my side in the grave.

O mio Fernando (Leonora, ACT III)

O mio Fernando, della terra il trono
a possederti avria donato il cor.

Ma puro l'amor mio come il perdono,
dannato, ahi lassa! è a disperato orror!
Il ver fia noto, e in tuo dispregio estremo,
la pena avrommi che maggior si de'.
Se il giusto tuo disdegno allor fia scemo,
piombi, gran Dio, la folgor tua su me.
Sù, crudeli! e chi v'arresta?

Scritto è in cielo il mio dolor!
Su, venite, ell'è una festa,
sparsa l'ara sia di fior.

Già la tomba a me s'appresta.

Ricoperta in negro vel
sia la trista fidanzata
che rejetta, disperata,
non avrà perdono in ciel.

O my Fernando, my heart would have given up
the kingdom of the earth in order to possess you.

But my unsullied love, like forgiveness,
is condemned, woe is me, to hopeless loathing.
The truth will be known, and in your extreme contempt
I shall have the punishment that is most fitting.
If your just disdain then lessens,

let your thunderbolt fall on me, great God.
Come, cruel ones! Who is stopping you?
My sorrow is inscribed in heaven!
Come, then, make a feast of it,
let flowers be scattered on the altar.
The grave is already being prepared for me.

Let the unhappy bride
be swathed in a black veil,
she who, rejected and despairing,
will find no forgiveness in heaven.

Spirto gentil (Fernando, ACT IV)

Spirto gentil, ne' sogni miei
brillasti un dì, ma ti perdei;

fuggi dal cor, mentita speme,
larve d'amor, fuggite insieme.
A te d'accanto del genitore,

scordavo il pianto, la patria, il ciel.

Tender spirit, in my dreams
you shone for a day, but I've lost you;

flee from my heart, lying hope;
ghosts of love, flee along with it.
At your side I forgot a father's weeping,

homeland, heaven.

Donna sleal! in tanto amore
segnasti il core d'onta mortal!

Spirto gentil (etc.).

"Faithless woman! In so great a love,
you marked my heart with deadly
    disgrace!
Tender spirit (etc.).

DON PASQUALE
(1843; libretto by the composer and Giovanni Ruffini, 1807–1881)

Quel guardo (Norina, ACT I)

"Quel guardo il cavaliere
in mezzo al cor trafisse;
piegò il ginocchio e disse:
Son vostro cavalier.
E tanto era in quel guardo
sapor di paradiso,
che il cavalier Riccardo,
tutto d'amor conquiso,
giurò che ad altra mai
non volgeria il pensier."

So anch'io la virtù magica
d'un guardo a tempo e loco,
so anch'io come si bruciano

i cori a lento foco:
D'un breve sorrisetto
conosco anch'io l'effetto,
di menzognera lagrima,
d'un subito languor;
conosco i mille modi
dell'amorose frodi,
i vezzi, e l'arti facili
per adescar un cor.
Ho testa bizzarra,
son pronta, vivace,
brillare mi piace,
mi piace scherzar;
se monto in furore
di rado sto al segno,
ma in riso lo sdegno
fo presto a cangiar.

"That look pierced the knight
in his heart of hearts;
he bent his knee and said:
'I am your knight.'
And in that look there was
such a flavor of heaven
that the knight Riccardo,
totally overcome by love,
swore he would never again
turn his thoughts to another
    woman."
I, too, know the magical power
of a timely glance in the right place;
I, too, know how hearts can be
    burned
over a slow fire:
I, too, understand the effect
of a quick little smile,
of a lying tear,
of sudden faintness;
I know the thousand ways
of lovers' deceptions,
the knacks, the easy methods
of entrapping a heart.
I'm giddy,
I'm ready-witted, I'm lively,
I love to sparkle,
I love to joke;
if I get furious
I seldom persist,
instead I quickly change
my anger into laughter.

Serenata: Com'è gentil (Ernesto [and Chorus], ACT III)

Com'è gentil	How soft
la notte a mezzo April!	the mid-April night is!
È azzurro il ciel,	The sky is blue,
la luna è senza vel:	the moon is unobscured:
Tutto è languor,	Everything is languidness,
pace, mistero, amor.	peace, mystery, love.
Ben mio, perchè	My love, why
ancor non vieni a me?	do you still not come to me?
Formano l'aure	The breezes form
d'amore accenti!	words of love!
Del rio nel mormore	In the murmur of the stream
sospiri senti—	you hear sighs—
Il tuo fedel	Your faithful lover
si strugge di desir;	is melting with longing;
Nina crudel,	cruel Nina,
mi vuoi veder morir!	you want to see me die!
Poi quando sarò morto,	Then when I'm dead,
piangerai,	you'll weep,
Ma richiamarmi in vita	but you won't be able
non potrai.	to bring me back to life!

Friedrich von Flotow (1812–1883)

MARTHA

(1847; libretto by "W. Friedrich" [Friedrich Wilhelm Riese], ca. 1805–1879; Italian translator unknown)

M'apparì (Lionel, ACT III)

Ove son io? Lo sento! A lei vicino!	Where am I? I feel it! Near her!
Arbitra ormai si fè del mio destino;	From now on she has become the master of my fate;
sfolgorante la veggio	I see her dazzling
del suo celeste e virginal sorriso,	with her heavenly and maidenly smile,
che mi cangia la terra in paradiso!	which changes earth into paradise for me!
M'apparì tutt'amor,	She appeared before me as love personified,
il mio sguardo l'incontrò;	my gaze fell upon her;

bella sì che il mio cor
ansioso a lei volò;
mi ferì, m'invaghì
quell'angelica beltà,
sculta in cor dall'amor
cancellarsi non potrà:
Il pensier di poter
palpitar con lei d'amor
può sopir il martir
che m'affanna e strazia il cor.

Marta, Marta, tu sparisti,

e il mio cor col tuo n'andò!
Tu la pace mi rapisti,

di dolor io morirò! (etc.)

she was so beautiful that my heart
flew to her, troubled;
that angelic beauty
wounded me, charmed me;
engraved in my heart by love,
it cannot be erased:
the thought of being able
to join her in the thrill of love
can soothe the pain
that afflicts me and torments my
heart.

Martha, Martha, you have vanished,
and my heart has gone with yours!
You've robbed me of my tranquility,
I shall die of sorrow! (etc.)

Umberto Giordano (1867–1948)

ANDREA CHÉNIER (1896; libretto by Luigi Illica, 1857–1919)

Un dì all'azzurro spazio (Chénier, ACT I)

Un dì all'azzurro spazio
guardai profondo,
e ai prati colmi di viole,

pioveva l'oro il sole
e folgorava d'oro
il mondo:
parea la terra un immane tesor,

e a lei serviva di scrigno, il firmamento.
Su dalla terra a la mia fronte
veniva una carezza viva, un bacio.
Gridai, vinto d'amor: T'amo,

tu che mi baci, divinamente
bella, o patria mia!
E volli pien d'amor

One day I looked deeply
at the blue expanse
and at the meadows filled with
violets;
the sun was showering gold,
and the world
was dazzling with gold:
earth seemed an enormous treasure
and the heavens were its jewel
box.
Up from the earth to my brow
came a lively caress, a kiss.
Overcome by love, I called out: "I
love you,
you that kiss me, divinely
beautiful, o my homeland!"
And filled with love, I wanted

pregar!
Varcai d'una chiesa la soglia;
là un prete ne le nicchie
dei santi e de la Vergine

accumulava doni ... e al sordo
  orecchio
un tremulo vegliardo invano

chiedeva pane e invan stendea la
  mano!
Varcai degli abituri l'uscio;
un uom vi calunniava bestem-
  miando
il suolo che l'erario a pena sazia
e contro Dio scagliava e contro gli
  uomini
le lagrime dei figli.
In cotanta miseria
la patrizia prole che fa?

Sol l'occhio vostro esprime umana-
  mente
qui un guardo di pietà,
ond'io guardato ho a voi così come
  a un angelo
e dissi:
Ecco la bellezza della vita!
Ma poi,
a le vostre parole,
un novello dolore
m'ha colto in pieno petto ...
O giovinetta bella, d'un poeta
non disprezzate il detto!
Udite! Non conoscete amor?
Amor, divino dono, non lo schernir,
del mondo anima e vita è l'amor!

to pray!
I crossed the threshold of a church;
there, in the niches
of the saints and the Virgin, a
  priest
was collecting donations ... and
  turned a deaf ear
to a quavering old man, asking in
  vain
for bread and holding out his hand
  in vain!
I crossed the doorway of the hovels;
there a man was cursing, railing at

the soil that barely paid his taxes,
and he was casting his children's
  tears
in the face of God and all mankind.
In so much misery,
what will become of this land's
  progeny?
Only your eye humanely shows

a kindly look of pity here,
and so I looked at you as at an
  angel
and said:
"Here is the beauty of life!"
But then,
at your words,
a fresh sorrow
struck me full in the breast ...
O lovely young girl, don't
despise a poet's word!
Listen! Don't you recognize love?
Love, divine gift, don't scorn it,
love is the soul and life of the
  universe!

Nemico della patria (Gérard, ACT III)

Nemico della patria?
È vecchia fiaba
che beatamente ancor la beve il
  popolo!

Enemy of the nation?
It's an old fable
that people still blissfully lap up!

Nato a Constantinopoli?
Straniero!
Studiò a Saint-Cyr?
Soldato!
Traditore!
Di Dumouriez un complice!
E poeta?
Sovvertitor di cuori e di costumi!

Un dì m'era di gioia passar
fra gli odi e le vendette, puro,
  innocente e forte!
Gigante mi credea!
Son sempre un servo!
Ho mutato padrone!
Un servo obbediente di violenta
  passione!
Ah, peggio! Uccido e tremo!
E mentre uccido, io piango!
Io della Redentrice figlio pel primo
  ho udito
il grido suo pel mondo ed ho al suo

il mio grido unito.
Or smarrita ho la fede nel sognato
  destino?
Com'era irradiato di gloria il mio
  cammino!
La coscienza nei cuori ridestar de
  le genti!
Raccogliere le lagrime dei vinti e
  sofferenti!
Fare del mondo un Pantheon! Gli
  uomini
in dii mutare
e in un sol bacio e abbraccio
tutte le genti amar . . .
Or io rinnego il santo grido!
Io d'odio ho colmo il core
e chi così m'ha reso, fiera ironia! È
  l'amore!
Sono un voluttuoso! Ecco il novo
  padrone:
Il senso! . . . Bugia tutto! Sol vero
  la passione!

Born in Constantinople?
"An alien!"
Studied at St. Cyr?
"A soldier!
A traitor!
An accomplice of Dumouriez!"
And a poet?
"A subverter of hearts and tradi-
  tions!"
Once it was my pleasure to pass,
pure, innocent and strong, among
  the hatreds and feuds!
I believed myself stupendous!
I'm still a servant!
I've changed masters!
An obedient slave to violent pas-
  sion!
Ah, worse yet! I kill and I tremble!
And while I'm killing, I weep!
I, a son of the Revolution from the
  outset, have heard
its call throughout the world, and
  have joined
my own cry with it.
Have I now lost faith in the goal
  I've dreamt of?
How illuminated by glory was my
  course!
To reawaken conscience in people's
  hearts!
To collect the tears of the van-
  quished and the suffering!
To make the world into a Pantheon!
  To change mankind
into gods,
and with a single kiss and embrace
to love all peoples . . .
Now I repudiate the holy cry!
My heart is brimful of hatred,
and what has changed me thus?—
  cruel irony! It is love!
I'm a voluptuary! There's my new
  master:
Sensuality! . . . Everything's a lie!
  Passion is the only truth!

La mamma morta (Maddalena, ACT III)

La mamma morta
m'hanno a la porta
della stanza mia;
moriva e mi salvava!
Poi, a notte alta, io con Bersi*
errava,
quando, ad un tratto, un livido
bagliore
guizza e rischiara innanzi a' passi
miei
la cupa via.
Guardo! Bruciava il loco di mia
culla!
Così fui sola!. . . E intorno il nulla!

Fame e miseria . . .
Il bisogno, il periglio . . .
Caddi malata! . . .
E Bersi, buona e pura,
di sua bellezza ha fatto
un mercato, un contratto per me!
Porto
sventura a chi bene mi vuole!

Fu in quel dolore
che a me venne l'amor!
Voce piena d'armonia
e dice: "Vivi ancora! Io son la vita!
Ne' miei occhi è il tuo cielo!
Tu non sei sola! Le lagrime tue
io le raccolgo! . . . Io sto sul tuo
cammino
e ti sorreggo!
Sorridi e spera! Io son l'amore!
Tutto intorno è sangue e fango?
Io son divino!
Io son l'oblio . . .
Io sono il dio
che sovra il mondo scende da
l'empireo,
fa della terra un ciel . . .
Ah! Io son l'amore!"

They killed my mother
at the door
of my room;
dying, she rescued me!
Then, in the depth of night, I was
wandering with Bersi
when, all of a sudden, a pale
glimmer
flickered to light up the gloomy
street
before me.
I looked! My birthplace was burning!
Thus I was alone!. . . And nothingness all around me!

Hunger and suffering . . .
The poverty, the danger . . .
I fell ill!
And Bersi, good and innocent,
sold her beauty,
made a bargain of it for my sake! I
bring
bad luck to whoever wishes me
well!

It was in the midst of that sorrow
that love came to me!
A melodious voice
saying: "Go on living! I am life!
Your heaven is in my eyes!
You are not alone! I collect
your tears! I will remain on your
path
and sustain you!
Smile and trust! I am love!
Are blood and filth all about you?
I am divine.
I am oblivion . . .
I am the god
who descends to the world from
the highest heaven
and makes of earth a paradise . . .
Ah! I am love!"

*Maddalena's maid.

Come un bel dì di maggio (Chénier, ACT IV)

Come un bel dì di maggio	Like a beautiful day in May
che con bacio di vento e carezza di raggio	that extinguishes itself in the heavens
si spegne in firmamento,	with a kiss of wind and caress of sunshine,
col bacio io d'una rima,	I, with the kiss of a rhyme,
carezza di poesia, salgo l'estrema cima	the caress of poetry, climb to the zenith
de l'esistenza mia.	of my existence.
La sfera che cammina	The sphere that strides
per ogni umana sorte ecco già mi avvicina	through all human destiny, see! it is already bringing me near
all'ora della morte,	to the hour of my death,
e forse pria che l'ultima	and perhaps, before my final
mia strofe sia finita, m'annuncierà il carnefice	stanza is finished, the executioner will proclaim to me
la fine della vita.	the end of my life!
Sia! Strofe, ultima Dea!	So be it! Stanza, last goddess!
Ancor dona al tuo poeta la sfolgorante idea,	Again grant to your poet the shining idea,
la fiamma consueta;	the customary fire;
io, a te, mentre tu vivida	on you, while you vividly
a me sgorghi dal cuore, darò per rima	spring from my heart, I'll bestow through rhyme
il gelido spiro	the icy breath
d'un uom che muore.	of a dying man.

Christoph Willibald von Gluck (1714–1787)

ORFEO ED EURIDICE
(1762; libretto by Raniero de Calzabigi, 1714–1795)

Che farò senza Euridice? (Orfeo, ACT III)

Che farò senza Euridice?	What shall I do without Eurydice?
Dove andrò senza il mio ben?	Where shall I go without my love?
Che farò? Dove andrò?	What shall I do? Where shall I go?
Che farò senza il mio ben?	What shall I do without my love?
Euridice! Euridice!	Eurydice! Eurydice!
Oh Dio! Rispondi! Rispondi!	Oh God! Answer! Answer!

Io son pure il tuo fedele.	I am still your faithful lover!
Ah! Non m'avanza,	Ah! I no longer have
più soccorso, più speranza,	any more help, any more hope,
nè dal mondo, nè dal ciel!	neither from earth nor from heaven!
Che farò (etc.).	What shall I do (etc.).

George Frideric Handel (1685-1759)

SERSE

(Xerxes; 1738; libretto adapted from Nicolò Minato, ca. 1630-1698)

Ombra mai fù (Serse, ACT I)

Ombra mai fù	There was never shade
di vegetabile	cast by a plant
cara ed amabile,	more dear and lovable
soave più.	and sweet.

Ruggiero Leoncavallo (1857-1919)

PAGLIACCI *(1892; libretto by the composer)*

Prologue: Si può? (Tonio)*

Si può? Si può? Signore! Signori! Scusatemi se da sol mi presento. Io sono il Prologo: Poichè in iscena ancor le antiche maschere mette l'autore, in parte ei vuol riprendere le vecchie usanze, e a voi di nuovo inviami. Ma non per dirvi come pria: "Le lacrime che noi versiam son false! Degli spasimi e de' nostri martir non allarmatevi!" No!

May I? May I? Ladies! Gentlemen! Pardon me for introducing myself. I am the Prologue: Because the author is putting the ancient mummers on stage again; in part, he wants to recapture old-fashioned customs and sends me to you again. But not in order to tell you, as of yore: "The tears we shed are counterfeit! Don't be alarmed

*In some sources this Prologue appears arbitrarily divided into short verselike lines, but there is no regular meter, and in other parts of the opera Leoncavallo clearly uses meter and rhyme in passages of poetry.

L'autore ha cercato invece pingervi uno squarcio di vita. Egli ha per massima sol che l'artista è un uom e che per gli uomini scrivere ei deve. Ed al vero ispiravasi.

Un nido di memorie in fondo a l'anima cantava un giorno, ed ei con vere lacrime scrisse, e i singhiozzi il tempo gli battevano! Dunque, vedrete amar sì come s'amano gli esseri umani; vedrete de l'odio i tristi frutti. Del dolor gli spasimi, urli di rabbia udrete, e risa ciniche!

E voi, piuttosto che le nostre povere gabbane d'istrioni, le nostr'anime considerate, poichè siam uomini di carne e d'ossa, e che di quest'orfano mondo al pari di voi spiriamo l'aere!

Il concetto vi dissi . . . Or ascoltate com'egli è svolto. Andiam! Incominciate!

by our pain and suffering!" No! The author has sought instead to paint a slice of life for you. His only guideline is that the artist is a man and that he should write for mankind. And he took his inspiration from reality.

One day, a nest of memories was singing in the depth of his soul, and he wrote with genuine tears, and his sobs marked the tempo! So, then, you will see loving, the way humans really love; You'll see the tragic fruits of hatred, the agony of sorrow, you'll hear screams of rage and cynical laughter!

And you, rather than our poor actors' costumes, consider our souls, since we are men of flesh and bone and breathe the air of this orphan world the same as you!

I've told you the idea . . . Now listen how it unfolds. Let's go! Begin!

Ballatella: Stridono lassù (Nedda, ACT I)

Oh! Che volo d'augelli, e quante strida!
Che chiedon? Dove van? Chissà
. . . La mamma

mia, che la buona ventura annunziava,
comprendeva il lor canto e a me bambina così cantava:

Hui! Stridono lassù, liberamente

lanciati a vol come frecce, gli augel.
Disfidano le nubi e 'l sol cocente,

Oh! What flocks of birds, and how they shriek!
What are they seeking? Where are they going? Who knows . . . My mother,

who was good at telling fortunes,

understood their song, and when I was a little girl, she would sing it to me thus:
Hui! The birds shriek up there, freely

hurled into flight, like arrows.
They challenge the clouds and the burning sun,

e vanno, e vanno per le vie del ciel.

Lasciateli vagar per l'atmosfera

questi assetati d'azzurro e splendor:

seguono anch'essi un sogno, una
chimera,
e vanno, e vanno fra le nubi d'or!

Che incalzi il vento e latri la
tempesta,
con l'ali aperte san tutto sfidar;

la pioggia, i lampi, nulla mai li
arresta,
e vanno, e vanno sugli abissi e i
mar.
Vanno laggiù verso un paese strano

che sognan forse e che cercano
invan.
Ma i boemi del ciel seguon l'arcano

poter che li sospinge . . . E van! E
van!

and travel, travel on the roads of
the sky.
Let them wander through the
atmosphere,
thirsting as they are for azure and
brightness:
they too are pursuing a dream, an
illusion,
and travel, travel among the golden
clouds!
Let the wind give chase and the
tempest howl,
with wings outspread, they face
every challenge;
the rain, the lightning, nothing
ever stops them,
and they travel, travel over chasms
and seas.
They travel over there, toward a
strange land
that perhaps they dream of and
seek in vain.
But the Gypsies of the sky follow
the mysterious
power that impels them . . . and
they travel, travel!

Vesti la giubba (Canio, ACT I)

Recitar! Mentre preso dal delirio

non so più quel che dico e quel che
faccio!
Eppur è d'uopo! sforzati . . .
Bah! sei tu forse un uom? Tu sei
Pagliaccio!
Vesti la giubba, e la faccia infarina.

La gente paga e rider vuole qua.

E se Arlecchin t'invola Colombina,

ridi, Pagliaccio e ognun applaudirà!

To perform! While, a prey to
delirium,
I no longer know what I'm saying
or doing!
And yet I must! Force yourself . . .
Bah! anyway, are you a man?
You're Pagliaccio [a clown]!
Dress up in your doublet, smear
flour on your face.
The people are paying and want to
laugh here.
And if Harlequin steals Columbine
from you,
laugh, Pagliaccio, and everyone
will applaud!

Tramuta in lazzi lo spasmo ed il pianto;
in una smorfia il singhiozzo e 'l dolor!
Ridi, Pagliaccio, sul tuo amore infranto!
Ridi del duol che t'avvelena il cor!

Turn your pain and weeping into comic gestures,
your sobs and sorrow into a funny grimace!
Laugh, Pagliaccio, about your shattered love!
Laugh at the pain that's poisoning your heart!

No! Pagliaccio non son (Canio, ACT II)

No! Pagliaccio non son; se il viso è pallido,
è di vergogna, e smania di vendetta!

L'uom riprende i suoi dritti, e il cor che sanguina
vuol sangue a lavar l'onta, o maledetta!
No! Pagliaccio non son! Son quei che stolido
ti raccolse orfanella in su la via

quasi morta di fame, e un nome offriati,
ed un amor ch'era febbre e follia!

[lines for Chorus & Silvio]
Sperai, tanto il delirio accecato m'aveva
se non amor, pietà . . . mercè!

Ed ogni sacrifizio
al cor lieto imponeva
e fidente credeva
più che in Dio stesso in te!
Ma il vizio alberga sol ne l'alma tua negletta;
tu viscere non hai, sol legge è 'l senso a te!
Va, non merti il mio duol, o meretrice abbietta,
vo' ne lo sprezzo mio schiacciarti sotto i piè!

No! I'm not Pagliaccio; if my face is pale,
it's from shame and a frenzy for revenge!
The man reasserts his rights, and the heart that bleeds
needs blood to cleanse its disgrace, o accursed woman!
No! I'm not Pagliaccio! I'm the man who stupidly
picked you, an orphan, off the street
when you were half dead from hunger, and offered you a name,
and a love that was fever and madness!

[lines for Chorus & Silvio]
My delirium had blinded me so much that I hoped
if not for love, for pity . . . for mercy!
And I imposed every sacrifice
on my heart gladly
and trusting believed
in you more than in God himself!
But only vice dwells in your abandoned soul;
you have no feelings, sex is your only law!
Go, you don't deserve my sorrow, you cheap whore,
in my contempt I'd like to crush you under my feet!

Pietro Mascagni *(1863–1945)*

CAVALLERIA RUSTICANA

(1890; libretto by Giovanni Targioni-Tozzetti, 1863–1934, and Guido Menasci, 1867–?)

Siciliana: O Lola (Turiddu)

(SICILIAN)
O Lola c'hai di latti la cammisa
si bianca e russa comu la cirasa,

quannu t'affacci fai la vucca a risa,

biatu pi lu primu cu ti vasa!

Ntra la puorta tua lu sangu è spasu,

ma nun me mpuorta si ce muoru
  accisu—
e si ce muoru e vaju'n paradisu
si nun ce truovo a ttia, mancu ce
  trasu.

(SICILIAN)
O Lola, in your milk-white shift,
you're as white and pink as cherry
  blossoms;
when you show yourself and make
  your lips smile,
he is most blessed who kisses you
  first!
Your doorstep is sprinkled with
  blood,
but I don't care if I die murdered
  there—
And if I die and go to heaven,
If I don't find you there I won't go
  in.

(ITALIAN)
O Lola, bianca come fior di spino,
quando t'affacci tu, s'affaccia il
  sole;
chi t'ha baciato il labbro porporino
grazia più bella a Dio chieder non
  vôle.
C'è scritto sangue sopra la tua
  porta,
ma di restarci a me non me n'importa;
se per te mojo e vado in paradiso,
non c'entro se non vedo il tuo bel
  viso.

(ITALIAN)
O Lola, white as hawthorn flowers,
when you show yourself, the sun
  comes out;
whoever's kissed your purple lips
won't ask God for a favor more
  lovely.
Blood is written over your door,

but I don't care if I'm killed there;

if I die for you and go to heaven,
I won't enter if I don't see your
  beautiful face.

Il cavallo scalpita (Alfio)

Il cavallo scalpita,
i sonagli squillano,
schiocca la frusta.—Ehi là!—
Soffii il vento gelido,
cada l'acqua e nevichi,
a me che cosa fa?
[CHORUS: O che bel mestiere
fare il carrettiere,
andar di qua e di là!]
M'aspetta a casa Lola,
che m'ama e mi consola,
ch'è tutta fedeltà.
Il cavallo scalpiti,
i sonagli squillino,
è Pasqua, ed io son qua!
O che (etc.) (WITH CHORUS)

The horse paws the ground,
the harness bells jangle,
the whip snaps.—Hey there!—
Let the icy wind blow,
let rain and snow fall,
what does it matter to me?
[CHORUS: Oh, what a fine trade
to be a carter,
to go here and there!]
Lola's waiting for me at home,
she loves me and comforts me,
she's totally faithful.
Let the horse paw the ground,
let the harness bells jangle,
it's Easter, and I'm here!
Oh, what (etc.) (WITH CHORUS)

Voi lo sapete (Santuzza)

Voi lo sapete, o mamma, prima
d'andar soldato
Turiddu aveva a Lola eterna fè
giurato.
Tornò, la seppe sposa; e con un
nuovo amore
volle spegner la fiamma che gli
bruciava il core.
M'amò, l'amai. Quell'invida d'ogni
delizia mia,

del suo sposo dimentica, arse di
gelosia.
Me l'ha rapito. Priva dell'onor mio
rimango:
Lola e Turiddu s'amano, io piango,
io piango.

O Mother, you know that, before
serving as a soldier,
Turiddu had sworn eternal love to
Lola.
He came back, he found her mar-
ried; and with a new love
he tried to quench the flame that
was burning his heart.
He loved me, I loved him. That
woman, envious of all my happiness,
forgetting her husband, burned
with jealousy.
She stole him from me. I am left
deprived of my honor:
Lola and Turiddu love each other, I
weep, I weep.

Viva il vino spumeggiante (Turiddu)

Viva il vino spumeggiante
nel bicchiere scintillante;

Long live the bubbling wine
in the sparkling glass;

come il riso dell'amante
mite infonde il giubilo!
Viva il vino ch'è sincero,
che ci allieta ogni pensiero,

e che annega l'umor nero
nell'ebbrezza tenera.
[many repeats, with Lola and
Chorus]

like a lover's laughter,
it gently inspires mirth!
Long live the wine that's pure,
that makes our every thought lighthearted,
and that drowns black moods
in loving intoxication.
[many repeats, with Lola and
Chorus]

Addio alla madre (Turiddu)

Mamma, quel vino è generoso, e certo
oggi troppi bicchier ne ho tracannato—
vado fuori all'aperto—
ma prima voglio che mi benedite

come quel giorno che partii soldato—
e poi—mamma, sentite—
s'io non tornassi—voi dovrete fare

da madre a Santa, ch'io le avea giurato
di condurla all'altare.
[LUCIA: Perchè parli così, figliuolo mio?]
Oh! nulla! È il vino che m'ha suggerito!
Per me pregate Iddio!
Un bacio, mamma! Un altro bacio! Addio!

Mother, this wine is strong, and surely
today I've gulped down too many glasses of it—
I'm going outside into the open—
But first I want you to give me your blessing
as on that day when I left for the army—
And then—Mother, listen—
in case I don't come back, you must be
a mother to Santa, because I had promised
to lead her to the altar.
[LUCIA: Why are you speaking this way, son?]
Oh! It's nothing! It's the wine that prompted me!
Pray to God for me!
A kiss, Mother! Another kiss! Goodbye!

Giacomo Meyerbeer (1791–1864)

L'AFRICANA

(L'Africaine; 1865; original French libretto by Eugène Scribe, 1791–1861, and François-Joseph Fétis, 1784–1871; Italian translator unknown)

O paradiso (Vasco, ACT IV)

O ridente suol . . . vago e bel giardin,
salute a voi, O Paradiso in terra!
Ciel azzur senza egual . . . che incantate il mio cor,
tu m'appartieni o nuovo mondo,
dono feci di te all'amato mio suolo natal.
A noi quest'apriche campagne!

A noi quest'incanto divin;
ricchi tesori! O meraviglie!
Ah, salute a voi! O bel paese!
Alfine mio sei tu . . . sì nuovo sol,

sì mio sei. O bel paese,
alfine mio sei tu!

O smiling earth . . . lovely, beautiful garden,
I greet you, o earthly Paradise!
Peerless blue sky . . . you that enchant my heart,
you belong to me, o new world,
I've made a gift of you to my beloved native land.
Ours will be this sunny countryside!

Ours this divine enchantment;
boundless riches! O wonders!
Ah, I greet you! O lovely land!
At last you're mine . . . this soil so new,
yes, you're mine. O lovely land,
at last you're mine!

Wolfgang Amadeus Mozart (1756–1791)

LE NOZZE DI FIGARO

(1786; libretto by Lorenzo Da Ponte, 1749–1838)

Se vuol ballare (Figaro, ACT I)

Bravo, signor padrone!
Ora incomincio a capir il mistero,
e a veder schietto
tutto il vostro progetto.
A Londra, è vero?

Bravo, master!
Now I begin to fathom the mystery,
and to see
your whole plan clearly.
To London, right?

Voi ministro, io corriero,
e la Susanna, segreta ambasciatrice.

You the envoy, I the messenger,
and Susanna the secret lady-
ambassador.

Non sarà, non sarà; Figaro il dice!

It won't happen, it won't happen;
Figaro says so!

Se vuol ballare,
Signor Contino,
il chitarrino
le suonerò.
Se vuol venire
nella mia scuola,
la capriola
le insegnerò.
Saprò, ma piano,
meglio ogni arcano
dissimulando
scoprir potrò.
L'arte schermendo,
l'arte adoprando,
di qua pungendo,
di là scherzando,
tutte le macchine
rovescierò.
Se vuol ballare (etc.).

If you wish to dance,
sir Count,
I'll play
the little guitar!
If you want to attend
my school,
I'll teach you
to caper.
I'll find out, but quietly,
by dissembling,
I'll be better able
to discover every secret.
By parrying cunning,
by using cunning,
by goading here,
by joking there,
I'll overturn
all your schemes.
If you wish (etc.).

Non so più (Cherubino, ACT I)

Non so più cosa son, cosa faccio,

I no longer know what I am, what
I'm doing;

or di foco, ora sono di ghiaccio,
ogni donna cangiar di colore,

first I'm afire, then I'm icy,
every woman makes me change
color,

ogni donna mi fa palpitar.

every woman makes my heart
pound.

Solo ai nomi d'amor, di diletto,

Just the words "love" and "pleasure"

mi si turba, mi s'altera il petto,
e a parlare mi sforza d'amore
un desio ch'io non posso spiegar.
Non so più (etc.).
Parlo d'amor vegliando,
parlo d'amor sognando,
all'acqua, all'ombra, ai monti,

disturb me, throw me into turmoil,
and I am driven to speak about love
by a longing I can't explain.
I no longer know (etc.).
Waking, I talk about love;
dreaming, I talk about love;
to the water, to the shade, to the
mountains,

ai fiori, all'erbe, ai fonti,

to the flowers, to the grass, to the
fountains,

all'eco, all'aria, ai venti,

che il suon de' vani accenti
portano via con sè.
E se non ho chi m'oda,

parlo d'amor con me!

to the echo, to the air, to the winds,
which carry away with them
the sound of my frivolous words.
And if there's no one to listen to me,
I talk about love to myself!

Non più andrai (Figaro, Act I)

Non più andrai, farfallone amoroso,
notte e giorno d'intorno girando,

delle belle turbando il riposo,

Narcisetto, Adoncino d'amor!
Non più avrai questi bei pennachini,
quel cappello leggiero e galante,
quella chioma, quell'aria brillante,

quel vermiglio donnesco color!
[much repetition of various phrases]
Tra guerrieri poffar Baccho!
Gran mustacchi, stretto sacco,
schioppo in spalla, sciabla al fianco,

collo dritto, muso franco,
o un gran casco, o un gran turbante,
molto onor, poco contante . . .
Ed invece del fandango
una marcia per il fango,
per montagne, per valloni,

colle nevi e i sollïoni,

al concerto di tromboni,
di bombarde, di cannoni,
che le palle in tutti i tuoni
all'orecchio fan fischiar.

[much repetition of earlier phrases]
Cherubino, alla vittoria,
alla gloria militar!

No longer will you gad about, amorous butterfly,
flitting around everywhere, night and day,
disturbing the rest of beautiful ladies,
little Narcissus, little loving Adonis!
You won't have that pretty plumage any longer,
that frivolous and dashing cap,
that mane of hair, that brilliant air,
that blushing, girlish complexion!
[much repetition of various phrases]
Among warriors, by Jove!
Long mustachios, straitened purse,
rifle at the shoulder, saber at the side,
neck held stiffly, bold expression,
either a big helmet or a big turban,
much honor, little cash . . .
And instead of the fandango,
a march through the mud,
through mountains, through canyons,
during snow and summer's dog-days,
to the sound of trombones,
of bombards, of cannons,
that make the bullets
whistle about your ears in every key.
[much repetition of earlier phrases]
Cherubino, off to victory,
off to military glory!

Porgi, amor (Countess, ACT II)

Porgi, amor, qualche ristoro	Love, offer me some solace
al mio duolo, a' miei sospir!	for my sorrow, for my sighs!
O mi rendi il mio tesoro,	Either restore my lover to me,
o mi lascia almen morir!	or at least let me die!

Voi che sapete (Cherubino, ACT II)

Voi che sapete	You, who know
che cosa è amor,	what love is like,
donne, vedete	ladies, see
s'io l'ho nel cor.	if I have it in my heart.
Quello ch'io provo,	That which I'm feeling,
vi ridirò,	I'll tell you again,
è per me nuovo,	it's new to me,
capir nol so.	I don't know what to make of it.
Sento un affetto	I feel a tenderness
pien di desir,	full of longing,
ch'ora è diletto,	that's sometimes a delight,
ch'ora è martir;	sometimes torment;
gelo, e poi sento	I freeze, and then I feel
l'alma avvampar,	my soul in flames,
e in un momento	and in a moment
torno a gelar.	I'm back to freezing.
Ricerco un bene	I'm seeking some happiness
fuori di me,	outside of myself,
non so chi il tiene,	I don't know who has it,
non so cos'è;	I don't know what it is;
sospiro e gemo	I sigh and groan
senza voler,	without meaning to,
palpito e tremo	I shiver and tremble
senza saper;	without knowing why;
non trovo pace	I have no peace
notte nè dì,	night or day,
ma pur mi piace	but still it's my pleasure
languir così.	to languish thus.
Voi che sapete	You who know
che cosa è amor,	what love is like,
donne, vedete	ladies, see
s'io l'ho nel cor.	if I have it in my heart.

Dove sono (Countess, ACT III)

Dove sono i bei momenti	Where are the precious moments
di dolcezza e di piacer?	of sweetness and delight?

Dove andaro i giuramenti
di quel labbro menzogner?
Perchè mai, se in pianti e in pene
per me tutto si cangiò,
la memoria di quel bene
dal mio sen non trapassò?
Dove sono (etc.)?
Ah! se almen la mia costanza
nel languire amando ognor,
mi portasse una speranza
di cangiar l'ingrato cor.

What became of the vows
from those lying lips?
Why, if everything has changed
into weeping and sorrow for me,
has the memory of that bliss
never passed from my breast?
Where are (etc.)?
Ah! If at least my constancy,
always loving, though I languish,
would bring me some hope
of changing that faithless heart!

Aprite un po' (Figaro, ACT IV)

Aprite un po' quegl'occhi,
uomini incauti e sciocchi,
guardate queste femmine,
guardate cosa son!
Queste chiamate dee
dagli ingannati sensi,
a cui tributa incensi
la debole ragion.
Son streghe che incantano
per farci penar,
sirene che cantano
per farci affogar,
civette che allettano
per trarci le piume,
comete che brillano
per toglierci il lume,
son rose spinose,
son volpi vezzose,
son orse benigne,
colombe maligne,
maestre d'inganni,
amiche d'affanni,
che fingono, mentono,
che amore non sentono,
non senton pietà.
Il resto non dico,
già ognuno lo sa.

Open your eyes a bit,
careless and foolish men!
Consider those women,
consider what they are!
These creatures called goddesses
by your deceived senses,
to whom your enfeebled reason
offers incense.
They're witches who enchant us
in order to make us suffer,
sirens who sing to us
in order to make us drown,
coquettes who seduce us
to pluck out our feathers,
comets that flash
to take away our own light;
they're thorny roses,
they're charming vixens,
they're harmless bears,
they're evil doves,
expert liars,
friends of anxiety,
who pretend, who lie,
who don't feel love,
don't feel pity.
I won't say the rest,
everyone already knows it.

Deh vieni, non tardar (Susanna, ACT IV)

Deh vieni, non tardar, o gioia bella!	Pray don't delay, o lovely joy!
Vieni ove amore per goder t'appella!	Come where love calls you to rejoice!
Finchè non splende in ciel notturna face,	Until the torch of night shines in the sky,
finchè l'aria è ancor bruna, e il mondo tace.	while the air is still dark and the world is silent.
Qui mormora il ruscel, qui scherza l'aura,	Here the brooklet murmurs, here the breezes play,
che col dolce sussurro il cor ristaura.	refreshing the heart with their sweet whispering.
Qui ridono i fioretti e l'erba è fresca,	Here the little flowers smile and the grass is fresh,
ai piaceri d'amor qui tutto adesca.	here everything beguiles one to love's pleasures.
Vieni, ben mio, tra queste piante ascose,	Come, my love, among these hidden trees,
Ti vo' la fronte incoronar di rose.	I want to crown your head with roses!

DON GIOVANNI
(1787; libretto by Lorenzo Da Ponte, 1749–1838)

Ah, chi mi dice mai (Donna Elvira, ACT I)

Ah, chi mi dice mai	Ah, whoever will tell me
quel barbaro dov'è,	where that cruel man is,
che per mio scorno amai,	whom I loved to my shame,
che mi mancò di fè?	who broke faith with me?
Ah! se ritrovo l'empio,	Ah! If I find the wretch,
e a me non torna ancor,	And he doesn't come back to me,
vo' farne orrendo scempio,	I'll massacre him horribly,
gli vo' cavar il cor!	I'll rip out his heart!
[repetitions with lines for Don Giovanni & Leporello]	[repetitions with lines for Don Giovanni & Leporello]

Madamina (Leporello, ACT I)

Madamina, il catalogo è questo delle belle che amò il padron mio;	Dear lady, This is the catalog of the beautiful women my master has loved,
un catalogo egli è che ho fatto io;	it's a catalog that I have made;

osservate, leggete con me!
In Italia seicento e quaranta;
in Almagna duecento e trent'una,

cento in Francia, in Turchia no-
    vant'una;
ma in Ispagna son già mille e tre!

V'han fra queste contadine,
cameriere, cittadine,
v'han contesse, baronesse,
marchesine, principesse,
e v'han donne d'ogni grado,
d'ogni forma, d'ogni età.
In Italia (etc.) . . . mille e tre!

Nella bionda egli ha l'usanza
di lodar la gentilezza,
nella bruna la costanza,
nella bianca la dolcezza.

Vuol d'inverno la grassotta,
vuol d'estate la magrotta.
È la grande maestosa,
la piccina è ognor vezzosa;
delle vecchie fa conquista
pel piacer di porle in lista.

Sua passion predominante
è la giovin principiante;
non si picca se sia ricca,
se sia brutta, se sia bella,

purchè porti la gonnella,
voi sapete quel che fa.

look at it, read it with me!
In Italy, six hundred and forty;
in Germany, two hundred and
    thirty-one;
one hundred in France, in Turkey
    ninety-one;
but in Spain there are already a
    thousand and three!
Among them are countrywomen,
chambermaids, city dwellers,
there are countesses, baronesses,
marchionesses, princesses,
and there are ladies of every rank,
of every shape, of every age.
In Italy (etc.) . . . a thousand and
    three!
With blondes, it's his practice
to praise their amiability,
with brunettes their fidelity,
with white-haired ones their
    sweetness.
In winter he wants them fat,
in summer he wants them thin.
The large woman is stately,
the tiny one is always charming;
He makes conquests of old women
for the pleasure of adding them to
    his list.
His chief passion
is the young beginner;
he doesn't insist that she be rich,
that she be ugly, that she be
    beautiful,
just as long as she wears a skirt
you know what he does.

Ah! fuggi il traditor! (Donna Elvira, ACT I)

Ah! fuggi il traditor!
Non lo lasciar più dir;
il labbro è mentitor,
fallace il ciglio!
Dai miei tormenti impara
a creder a quel cor;
e nasca il tuo timor
dal mio periglio.

Ah! fly from the betrayer!
Don't let him say any more;
his lips lie,
his brow deceives!
Learn from my suffering
to trust in that heart;
and let your fear be born
from my peril.

Or sai chi l'onore (Donna Anna, ACT I)

Or sai chi l'onore	Now you know who
rapire a me volse,	tried to steal my virtue,
che fu il traditore,	who was the betrayer,
che il padre mi tolse.	who deprived me of my father.
Vendetta ti chiedo,	I ask vengeance of you,
la chiede il tuo cor.	your heart asks it.
Rammenta la piaga	Remember the wound
del misero seno,	in his pitiful breast,
rimira di sangue	recall the ground
coperto il terreno,	covered with blood,
se l'ira in te langue	should the frenzy of a just rage
d'un giusto furor!	languish in you!

Dalla sua pace (Don Ottavio, ACT I)

Dalla sua pace la mia dipende,	My tranquility depends on hers,
quel che a lei piace vita mi rende,	what gives her pleasure restores life to me,
quel che lei incresce morte mi dà.	what grieves her kills me.
S'ella sospira, sospiro anch'io,	If she sighs, I sigh too,
è mia quell'ira, quel pianto è mio;	that rage is mine, those tears are mine;
e non ho bene s'ella non l'ha!	and I have no happiness if she has none!

Finch'han dal vino ("Champagne Aria"; Don Giovanni, ACT I)

Finch'han dal vino	Have a grand party
calda la testa,	prepared
una gran festa	till their heads grow hot
fa preparar!	with wine!
Se trovi in piazza	If you find some girl
qualche ragazza,	in the town square,
teco ancor quella	try to bring her
cerca menar.	along too.
Senza alcun ordine	Let there be dancing
la danza sia,	in no set order,
chi'l minuetto,	let some dance
chi la follia,	the minuet,
chi l'alemana	some the folia,
farai ballar!	some the allemande!
Ed io frattanto	And meanwhile,
dall'altro canto	on the other hand,
con questa e quella	I'll make love

vo' amoreggiar.	to this girl and that.
Ah, la mia lista	Ah, by tomorrow morning
doman mattina	you must increase
d'una decina	my list
devi aumentar!	by ten or so!

Batti, batti (Zerlina, ACT I)

Batti, batti, o bel Masetto,	O handsome Masetto, hit, hit
la tua povera Zerlina:	your poor Zerlina:
starò qui come agnellina	I'll stand here like a little lamb
le tue botte ad aspettar.	and await your blows.
Lascerò straziarmi il crine,	I'll let you pull out my hair,
lascerò cavarmi gli occhi;	I'll let you rip out my eyes;
e le care tue manine	then I'll still happily kiss
lieta poi saprò baciar.	your dear little hands.
Ah, lo vedo, non hai core.	Ah, I see, you haven't the heart.
Pace, pace, o vita mia!	Peace, peace, o my life!
in contento ed allegria	In contentment and joy
notte e dì vogliam passar.	we'll spend our nights and days.

Deh vieni alla finestra (Don Giovanni, ACT II)

Deh vieni alla finestra, o mio tesoro,	Pray, come to the window, o my treasure,
deh vieni a consolar il pianto mio.	pray, come to console my tears.
Se neghi a me di dar qualche ristoro,	If you refuse to give me some relief,
davanti agli occhi tuoi morir vogl'io!	I'll die before your eyes!
Tu ch'hai la bocca dolce più che miele,	You, whose mouth is sweeter than honey,
tu che il zucchero porti in mezzo al core,	you, who bring sweetness to the depths of my heart.
non esser, gioia mia, con me crudele!	Don't be cruel to me, my joy.
Lasciati almen veder, mio bell'amore!	At least show yourself, my beautiful love!

Vedrai, carino (Zerlina, ACT II)

Vedrai, carino,	You'll see, dearest,
se sei buonino,	if you're a good boy,
che bel rimedio ti voglio dar.	what a lovely remedy I'll give you.
È naturale,	It's natural,
non da disgusto,	it won't make you sick,

e lo speziale non lo sa far.	and the pharmacist doesn't know how to make it.
È un certo balsamo	It's a certain balm
che porto addosso,	that I carry around,
dare tel posso,	I can give you some
se il vuoi provar.	if you want to try it.
Saper vorresti	Do you want to know
dove mi sta?	where I keep it?
Sentilo battere,	Feel it beating,
toccami qua!	touch me here!

Il mio tesoro (Don Ottavio, ACT II)

Il mio tesoro intanto	In the meantime,
andate a consolar!	go to comfort my beloved!
E del bel ciglio il pianto	And try to dry the tears
cercate di asciugar.	from her lovely lashes.
Ditele che i suoi torti	Tell her that I'm going
a vendicar io vado;	to avenge her wrongs;
che sol di stragi e morti	that I'll return only
nunzio vogl'io tornar!	as messenger of destruction and death!

Mi tradì (Donna Elvira, ACT II)

In quali eccessi, o Numi!	In what excesses, o gods!
in quai misfatti orribili, tremendi,	in what horrible, tremendous crimes
è avvolto il sciagurato!	the wretched man is involved!
Ah no, non puote tardar l'ira del cielo,	Oh no, the wrath of heaven cannot delay,
la giustizia tardar.	justice cannot delay.
Sentir già parmi la fatale saetta,	I seem already to hear the fatal thunderbolt
che gli piomba sul capo!	falling on his head!
Aperto veggio il baratro mortal.	I see the deadly abyss gaping.
Misera Elvira!	Unhappy Elvira!
Che contrasto d'affetti in sen ti nasce!	What a clash of emotions wells up in your breast!
Perché questi sospiri e queste ambascie?	Why these sighs and this anguish?
Mi tradì quell'alma ingrata,	That ungrateful soul betrayed me,
infelice o Dio, mi fa!	he makes me wretched, o God!
Ma tradita e abbandonata	But betrayed and abandoned,
provo ancor per lui pietà.	I yet feel pity for him.

Quando sento il mio tormento,	When I feel my torment,
di vendetta il cor favella,	my heart speaks of revenge,
ma se guardo il suo cimento,	but if I consider his peril,
palpitando il cor mi va.	it makes my heart pound.

Non mi dir (Donna Anna, ACT II)

Non mi dir, bell'idol mio,	Don't tell me, my handsome beloved,
che son io crudel con te,	that I am cruel to you;
tu ben sai quant'io t'amai,	you well know how much I've loved you,
tu conosci la mia fè.	you recognize my faithfulness.
Calma, calma il tuo tormento,	Calm, calm your suffering
se di duol non vuoi ch'io mora.	if you don't want me to die of sorrow.
Forse, forse un giorno il cielo ancora	Perhaps, perhaps one day heaven will yet
sentirà pietà di me!	have pity on me!

COSÌ FAN TUTTE
(1790; libretto by Lorenzo Da Ponte, 1749–1838)

Smanie implacabili (Dorabella, ACT I)

Ah! Scostati! Paventa il tristo effetto	Ah! Begone! Beware the doleful aftermath
d'un disperato affetto!	of a desperate passion!
Chiudi quelle finestre; odio la luce,	Close those windows; I hate the light,
odio l'aria che spiro, odio me stessa.	I hate the air I breathe, I hate my very self.
Chi schernisce il mio duol, chi mi consola?	Who scoffs at my sorrow, who comforts me?
Deh, fuggi, per pietà! Lasciami sola!	Pray run away, for pity's sake! Leave me alone!
Smanie implacabili	Relentless frenzies
che m'agitate,	that torment me,
entro quest'anima	you no longer subside
più non cessate	within my mind
finchè l'angoscia	until the anxiety
mi fa morir.	kills me.
Esempio misero	If I live,
d'amor funesto	I'll give the Furies

darò all'Eumenidi,
se viva resto,
col suono orribile
de' miei sospir.

a wretched example
of a distressing love,
with the fearful sound
of my sighs.

Come scoglio (Fiordiligi, ACT I)

Temerari! Sortite!
Fuori di questo loco!
E non profani

l'alito infausto degli infami detti
nostro cor, nostro orecchio e nostri affetti!
Invan per voi, per gli altri, invan si cerca
le nostr'alme sedur; l'intatta fede

che per noi già si diede ai cari amanti,
saprem loro serbar infino a morte

a dispetto del mondo e della sorte.
Come scoglio immoto resta
contro i venti e la tempesta,
così ognor quest'alma è forte
nella fede e nell'amor.
Con noi nacque quella face,
che ci piace
e ci consola,
e potrà la morte sola
far che cangi affetto il cor.
Rispettate,
anime ingrate,
questo esempio di costanza,
e una barbara speranza
non vi renda audaci ancor.

Rash men! Depart!
Away from this spot!
And may the ill-omened breath of infamous words
not profane
our hearts, our ears and our affections!
In vain for you, for others, in vain is the attempt
to seduce our souls; the intact fidelity
already given by us to our dear sweethearts
we shall be able to preserve for them until death
in despite of the world and fate.
As a rock remains unmoved
when assailed by winds and storm,
thus this soul is strong forever
in its fidelity and in its love.
That light was born within us
which pleases us
and comforts us,
and only death will make
our hearts alter their affection.
Respect,
thankless spirits,
this example of constancy,
and do not let your cruel hopes
embolden you further.

Un'aura amorosa (Ferrando, ACT I)

Cosa serve? A battaglia finita

fia la cena per noi più saporita.

Un'aura amorosa

What's the use? When the battle is over
the dinner will be all the tastier for us.

A loving breath

del nostro tesoro
un dolce ristoro
al cor porgerà;
al cor che, nudrito
da speme d'amore,
d'un'esca migliore
bisogno non ha.
Un'aura amorosa (etc.).

from my sweetheart
will bring sweet refreshment
to my heart;
to my heart that, feeding
on the hope of love,
has no need
of better fuel.
A loving breath (etc.).

Amilcare Ponchielli (1834–1886)

LA GIOCONDA
(1876; libretto by "Tobia Gorrio" [Arrigo Boito], 1842–1918)

Cielo e mar (Enzo, ACT II)

Cielo e mar! L'etereo velo
splende come un santo altar.
L'angiol mio verrà dal cielo?
L'angiol mio verrà dal mare?
Qui l'attendo, ardente spira
oggi il vento dell'amor.
Ah, quell'uom che vi sospira
vi conquide, oh sogni d'or!

Per l'aura fonda
non appar nè suol nè monte:

l'orizzonte bacia l'onda,
l'onda bacia l'orizzonte!
Qui nell'ombra ov'io mi giacio
coll'anelito del cor,
vieni, oh donna, vieni al bacio
della vita e dell'amor.
Vieni, oh donna, qui t'attendo
coll'anelito del cor (etc.).

Sky and sea! The veil of heaven
glows like a holy altar.
Will my angel come from the sky?
Will my angel come from the sea?
I await her here, love's breeze
blows ardently today.
Ah, that man who sighs for you
will vanquish you, oh dreams of
love!
Through the dense atmosphere
neither earth nor mountain appears:
The horizon kisses the waves,
the waves kiss the horizon!
Here in the shade where I'm lying
with yearning heart,
come, oh lady, come to the kiss
of life and of love.
Come, oh lady, I wait for you here
with a yearning heart (etc.).

Suicidio! (Gioconda, ACT IV)

Suicidio!
In questi fieri momenti
tu sol mi resti e il cor mi tenti.

Suicide!
During these harsh moments
you alone remain with me and
tempt my heart.

Ultima voce del mio destino,	The final voice of my fate,
ultima croce del mio cammin.	the last hurdle on my life's journey.
E un dì leggiadre volavan l'ore!	And once the hours flew by lightly!
Perdei la madre, perdei l'amore,	I've lost my mother, I've lost my love,
vinsi l'infausta gelosa febbre . . .	I've vanquished the hapless fever of jealousy . . .
Or piombo esausta fra le tenebre!	Now I fall exhausted among the shadows!
Tocco alla meta . . . domando al ciel	I've reached my objective . . . I beg heaven
di dormir queta dentro l'avel.	that I may sleep silently in my tomb.

Giacomo Puccini (1858–1924)

MANON LESCAUT

(1893; libretto by Luigi Illica, 1857–1919, Giuseppe Giacosa, 1847–1906, Giulio Ricordi, 1840–1912, Marco Praga, Domenico Oliva et al.)

Donna non vidi mai (Des Grieux, ACT I)

Donna non vidi mai simile a questa!	I've never seen a woman like this one!
A dirle: io t'amo,	Telling her "I love you,"
a nuova vita l'alma mia si desta.	my soul awakens to new life.
"Manon Lescaut mi chiamo!"	"My name is Manon Lescaut!"
Come queste parole profumate	How these fragrant words
mi vagan nello spirto	roam through my mind
e ascose fibre vanno a carezzare.	and start to arouse hidden depths of emotion.
O sussurro gentil, deh! Non cessare!	O delightful whisper, pray don't stop!

In quelle trine morbide (Manon, ACT II)

È ver! L'ho abbandonato	It's true! I left him
senza un saluto . . . un bacio!	without a goodbye . . . or a kiss!
In quelle trine morbide	Amid this soft lace
nell'alcova dorata v'è un silenzio	in the gilded alcove, there's a
gelido mortal, v'è un silenzio,	cold deadly silence, there's a silence,
un freddo che m'agghiaccia!	a chill that freezes me!

Ed io che m'ero avvezza
a una carezza
voluttuosa
di labbra ardenti e d'infuocate
   braccia . . .
or ho . . . tutt'altra cosa!

O mia dimora umile,
tu mi ritorni innanzi
gaia, isolata, bianca
come un sogno gentile
e di pace e d'amor!

And I, who had grown accustomed
to a sensual
caress
from ardent lips and eager arms
   . . .
Now I have . . . something entirely
   different!

O my humble dwelling,
you reappear before me
happy, secluded, white
like a sweet dream
of peace and love!

LA BOHÈME

(1896; libretto by Luigi Illica, 1857–1919, and Giuseppe Giacosa, 1847–1906)

Che gelida manina (Rodolfo, ACT I)

Che gelida manina,
se la lasci riscaldar.
Cercar che giova?
Al buio non si trova.

What an ice-cold little hand,
won't you let me warm it?
What's the use of searching?
We won't find it [the lost key] in
   the dark.

Ma per fortuna
è una notte di luna
e qui la luna
l'abbiamo vicina.
Aspetti, signorina,
le dirò con due parole
chi son, e che faccio,
come vivo. Vuole?
Chi son? Sono un poeta.
Che cosa faccio? Scrivo.
E come vivo? Vivo.
In povertà mia lieta
scialo da gran signore
rime e inni d'amore.
Per sogni e per chimere
e per castelli in aria
l'anima ho milionaria.
Talor dal mio forziere
ruban tutti i gioielli
due ladri: gli occhi belli.

But luckily,
it's a moonlit night
and up here we have
the moon near us.
Wait, Miss,
and I'll tell you in a couple of words
who I am, and what I do,
how I live. Would you like that?
Who am I? I'm a poet.
What do I do? I write.
And how do I live? I live.
In my merry poverty
like a great lord I squander
poems and hymns of love.
For dreams and fantasies
and castles in the air
I have the soul of a millionaire.
Occasionally all the gems
are stolen from my strongbox
by two thieves: beautiful eyes.

V'entrar con voi pur ora,	Just now they came in with you,
ed i miei sogni usati,	and my worn-out dreams,
e i bei sogni miei	my lovely dreams,
tosto si dileguar!	quickly faded!
Ma il furto non m'accora	But the theft doesn't distress me
poichè v'ha preso stanza	because in its place
la [dolce] speranza!	there's such [a pleasant] hope!
Or che mi conoscete,	Now that you know me,
parlate voi, deh!	you speak, I beg you!
Parlate! Chi siete?	Speak! Who are you?
Vi piaccia dir!	Please tell me!

Mi chiamano Mimì (Mimì, ACT I)

Sì. Mi chiamano Mimì,	Yes. They call me Mimì,
ma il mio nome è Lucia.	but my name is Lucia.
La storia mia	My story
è breve. A tela o a seta	is short. I embroider linen or silk
ricamo in casa e fuori.	in my home and outside.
Son tranquilla e lieta	I'm contented and happy,
ed è mio svago	and enjoy
far gigli e rose.	making lilies and roses.
Mi piaccion quelle cose	I like those things
che han sì dolce malia,	that possess such sweet enchant-
	ment,
che parlano d'amor, di primavere,	that speak of love, of springtimes,
che parlano di sogni e di chimere—	that speak of dreams and fancies—
quelle cose che han nome poesia.	those things called poetry.
Lei m'intende?	Do you understand me?
[RODOLFO: Sì.]	[RODOLFO: Yes.]
Mi chiamano Mimì,	They call me Mimì,
il perchè non so.	I don't know why.
Sola mi fo	I make
il pranzo da me stessa.	dinner for myself alone.
Non vado sempre a messa	I don't always go to Mass,
ma prego assai il Signor.	but I often pray to God.
Vivo sola, soletta,	I live alone, all alone,
là in una bianca cameretta:	in a little white room over there.
guardo su i tetti e in cielo,	I have a view over the roofs and
	into the sky,
ma quando vien lo sgelo	but when it thaws,
il primo sole è mio—	I get the first sunshine—
il primo bacio dell'aprile è mio!	April's first kiss is mine!
il primo sole è mio!	The first sunshine is mine!
Germoglia	A rose
in un vaso una rosa.	blooms in a vase.

Foglia a foglia	I sniff it
la spiro! Così gentil	petal by petal! How lovely
il profumo d'un fior!	is the fragrance of a flower!
Ma i fior ch'io faccio, ahimè,	But the flowers that I make, alas!
non hanno odore!	have no smell!
Altro di me non le saprei narrare:	I don't know what else to tell you about myself:
sono la sua vicina	I'm your neighbor
che la vien fuori d'ora	who comes at this late hour
a importunare.	to bother you.

Quando men vo (Musetta, ACT II)

Quando men vo,	When I pass by,
quando men vo soletta per la via,	when I pass by alone on the street,
la gente sosta e mira,	people stop and stare,
e la bellezza mia tutta ricerca in me,	and examine all my beauty
da capo a piè—	from head to foot—
[Marcello & Alcindoro each sing one line]	[Marcello & Alcindoro each sing one line]
ed assaporo allor la bramosia	and then I relish the acute desire
sottil che dagl'occhi traspira	which they show in their eyes
e dai palesi vezzi intender sa	and which from the evident attractions can intuit
alle occulte beltà.	the hidden beauties.
Così l'effluvio del desio	And so the outpouring of longing
tutta m'aggira,	surrounds me,
felice mi fa.	delights me!

Donde lieta uscì (Mimì, ACT III)

Donde lieta uscì al tuo grido	Mimì returns alone
d'amore torna sola	to the solitary nest
Mimì al solitario nido.	she lightheartedly left at your loving call.
Ritorna un'altra volta	She returns once more
a intesser finti fior.	to weave artificial flowers.
Addio senza rancor.	Goodbye, with no hard feelings.
Ascolta, ascolta.	Listen, listen.
Le poche robe aduna che lasciai sparse.	Gather up the few things that I left scattered about.
Nel mio cassetto stan chiusi	Locked in my drawer
quel cerchietto d'or,	are that golden ring
e il libro di preghiere.	and my prayerbook.
Involgi tutto quanto in un grembiale,	Wrap them all up in an apron,

manderò il portiere.	I'll send the porter round.
Bada—sotto il guanciale	Listen!—under the pillow
c'è la cuffietta rosa.	is the pink bonnet.
Se vuoi serbarla a ricordo d'amor!	You may want to save it as a memento of our love!
Addio, addio senza rancor!	Goodbye, goodbye with no hard feelings!

Vecchia zimarra (Colline, ACT IV)

Vecchia zimarra, senti,	Listen, old overcoat,
io resto al pian,	I'm staying at ground level,
tu ascendere	you must now climb
il sacro monte or devi.	the sacred mountain.*
Le mie grazie ricevi.	Accept my thanks.
Mai non curvasti il logoro	Never have you bent your thread-bare
dorso ai ricchi ed ai potenti.	back to the rich and to the power-ful.
Passar nelle tue tasche	Poets and philosophers
come in antri tranquilli	have spent time in your pockets,
filosofi e poeti.	as in tranquil grottoes.
Ora che i giorni lieti	Now that these happy days
fuggir, ti dico addio,	are gone, I bid you farewell,
fedele amico mio,	my faithful friend,
addio, addio.	farewell, farewell.

*Slang for pawnshop.

TOSCA

(1900; libretto by Giuseppe Giacosa, 1847–1906, and Luigi Illica, 1857–1919)

Recondita armonia (Cavaradossi, ACT I)

Recondita armonia	The hidden harmony
di bellezze diverse! . . . È bruna Floria	in contrasting beauties! . . . Floria,
l'ardente amante mia,	my fiery lover, is brunette,
[SACRISTAN: Scherza coi fanti e lascia star i santi.]	[SACRISTAN: He makes merry with lowlifes and neglects the saints.]
e te, beltade ignota	and you, unknown beauty,
cinta di chiome bionde!	are encircled by blonde hair!

Tu azzurro hai l'occhio,	You have blue eyes,
Tosca ha l'occhio nero!	Tosca's eyes are dark!
[SACRISTAN: (same line as above)]	[SACRISTAN: (same line as above)]
L'arte nel suo mistero	Art in its mystery
le diverse bellezze insiem confonde:	mixes together the different kinds of beauty:
ma nel ritrar costei	but while I paint her,
il mio solo pensier, } (WITH	I think only of you, } (WITH
Tosca sei tu!* } SACRISTAN)	Tosca! } SACRISTAN)

*In the original libretto, "tu sei," rhyming with "costei."

Vissi d'arte (Tosca, ACT II)

Vissi d'arte, vissi d'amore,	I have lived for art, I have lived for love,
non feci mai male ad anima viva!	I've never harmed a living soul!
Con man furtiva	With a clandestine touch,
quante miserie conobbi, aiutai.	I've eased such unhappiness as I've known about.
Sempre con fè sincera	Always with true faith
la mia preghiera	my prayers
ai santi tabernacoli salì.	have ascended to the holy tabernacles.
Diedi fiori agli altar.	I've given flowers for the altars.
Nell'ora del dolore	In the hour of sorrow,
perchè, Signore,	why, Lord,
perchè mi rimuneri così?	why do you repay me thus?
Diedi gioielli	I've given jewels
della Madonna al manto,	for the Madonna's robes,
e diedi il canto	and I've given my songs
agli astri, al ciel,	to the stars, to the heavens,
che ne ridean più belli.	which smiled more beautifully as a result.
Perchè, Signore (etc.)?	Why, Lord (etc.)?

E lucevan le stelle (Cavaradossi, ACT III)

E lucevan le stelle ed olezzava	And the stars were shining and the earth
la terra, stridea l'uscio	was fragrant, and the garden gate
dell'orto, e un passo sfiorava la rena.	creaked, and footsteps brushed over the sand.
Entrava ella, fragrante,	She entered, perfumed,
mi cadea fra le braccia.	and fell into my arms.

Oh! Dolci baci, o languide carezze,	Oh! Sweet kisses, o leisurely caresses,
mentr'io fremente	while, trembling, I
le belle forme disciogliea dai veli!	freed her beautiful body from its garments!
Svanì per sempre il sogno mio d'amore . . .	My dream of love has disappeared forever . . .
L'ora è fuggita	The hour has flown
e muoio disperato! . . .	and I die without hope! . . .
E non ho amato mai tanto la vita!	And never have I loved life so much!

MADAMA BUTTERFLY

(1904; libretto by Luigi Illica, 1857–1919, and Giuseppe Giacosa, 1847–1906)

Un bel dì (Butterfly, ACT II)

Un bel dì vedremo	One fine day we'll see
levarsi un fil di fumo	a thread of smoke rising
sull'estremo confin del mare.	on the ocean's farthest edge.
E poi la nave appare.	And then the ship appears.
Poi la nave bianca	Then the white ship
entra nel porto,	sails into port,
romba il suo saluto.	thundering its salute.
Vedi? È venuto!	You see? He's come!
Io non gli scendo incontro, io no.	I won't go down to meet him, not I.
Mi metto	I'll place myself
là sul ciglio del colle e aspetto, aspetto	there, on the brow of the hill, and wait, wait
gran tempo e non mi pesa	a great while, and I won't be bored
la lunga attesa.	by the long wait.
È uscito dalla folla cittadina	Issuing from the crowd of towns-people,
un uomo, un picciol punto	a man, a little dot,
s'avvia per la collina.	is moving up the hill.
Chi sarà? Chi sarà?	Who can it be? Who can it be?
E come sarà giunto	And as he's arriving,
che dirà? Che dirà?	what will he say? What will he say?
Chiamerà "Butterfly" dalla lontana.	From afar he'll call, "Butterfly."
Io senza far riposta	Without answering,
me ne starò nascosta	I'll hide
un po' per celia, e un po' per non morire	partly for fun, and partly so I won't die

al primo incontro, ed egli alquanto in pena	at the first meeting, and he, a little miffed,
chiamerà, chiamerà:	will call, will call,
"Piccina mogliettina,	"Little wife,
olezzo di verbena!"	fragrance of verbena!"—
i nomi che mi dava al suo venire.	the names that he gave me when he first came.
Tutto questo avverrà, te lo prometto.	All this will happen, I promise you;
Tienti la tua paura,	keep your fear to yourself,
io con sicura	with firm
fede l'aspetto.	faith I await him.

Addio fiorito asil (Pinkerton, ACT III)*

Addio fiorito asil	Farewell, flowery haven
di letizia e d'amor,	of gaiety and love,
sempre il mito tuo sembiante	I shall always see your gentle face
con strazio atroce vedrò.	with dreadful pain.
[two lines for Sharpless]	[two lines for Sharpless]
Addio fiorito asil,	Farewell, flowery haven,
non reggo al tuo squallor!	I can't bear your desolation!
Fuggo, fuggo—son vil.	I'll run away, I'll run away—I'm despicable!
[a line for Sharpless]	[a line for Sharpless]

*The text given here matches the definitive score and standard performance practice. Puccini, who frequently altered his librettists' work, has here left no trace of the original rhyme scheme. In the opera, this "aria" is actually a duet with Sharpless.

Tu? tu? piccolo Iddio! (Butterfly, ACT III)

Tu? tu? piccolo Iddio!	You? you? little god!
Amore, amore mio,	My love, my love,
fior di giglio e di rosa.	blossom of lily and rose.
Non saperlo mai	Don't ever find out
per te, pei tuoi puri	that for you, for your innocent
occhi, muor Butterfly,	eyes, Butterfly is dying,
perchè tu possa andare	so that you can go
di là dal mare	across the sea
senza che ti rimorda ai dì maturi,	and have no regret after you're grown up
il materno abbandono.	because your mother abandoned you.
O a me, sceso dal trono	O you, who have come down to me from the throne
dell'alto Paradiso,	of high heaven,

guarda ben fiso, fiso	look steadfastly, steadfastly
di tua madre la faccia! . . .	at your mother's face! . . .
che ten resti una traccia,	so that some trace of it will stay with you,
guarda ben! Amore, addio!	take a good look. My love, goodbye!
Addio, piccolo amor!	Goodbye, little love!
Va. Gioca, gioca.	Go. Play, play.

LA FANCIULLA DEL WEST

(1910; libretto by Carlo Zangarini, 1874–1943, and Guelfo Civinini [dates unavailable])

Ch'ella mi creda (Johnson, ACT III)

Risparmiate lo scherno . . . Della morte	Spare your mockery . . . I'm not worried
non mi metto pensiero: e ben voi tutti	about death: and all of you
lo sapete! Pistola o laccio è uguale.	are well aware of it! Pistol or noose, it's all the same.
Se mi sciogliete un braccio,	If you untie one arm
mi sgozzo di mia mano! . . .	I'll cut my own throat! . . .
D'altro voglio parlarvi:	It's something else I want to talk to you about:
della donna ch'io amo . . .	the woman I love . . .
[lines for 7 other characters and Chorus]	[lines for 7 other characters and Chorus]
(Ti ringrazio, Sonora!)	(Thanks, Sonora!)
Per lei, per lei soltanto,	For her, only for her,
che tutti amate,	whom you all love,
a voi chiedo una grazia e una promessa . . .	I ask you for a favor and a promise . . .
Ch'ella non sappia mai come son morto!	That she never learns how I died!
[one line for Rance]	[one line for Rance]
Ch'ella mi creda libero e lontano,	Let her believe me free and far away,
sopra una nuova via di redenzione! . . .	on a new path of redemption! . . .
Aspetterà ch'io torni . . .	She'll wait for me to come back . . .
E passeranno i giorni,	And the days will pass,
ed io non tornerò . . .	and I won't return . . .
Minnie, della mia vita mio solo fiore,	Minnie, my life's only blossom,
Minnie che m'hai voluto tanto bene! . . .	Minnie who loved me so much! . . .

LA RONDINE *(1917; libretto by Giuseppe Adami, 1878–1946)*

Chi il bel sogno di Doretta (Prunier & Magda, ACT I)*

PRUNIER: Chi il bel sogno di Doretta
potè indovinar?
Il suo mistero nessuno mai scoprì!
Un bel giorno il re la bimba
volle avvicinar:
"Se tu a me credi,
se tu a me cedi,
ti farò ricca!
Ah! creatura!
Dolce incanto!
La vana tua paura,
il tepido tuo pianto
ora sparirà!"
"No, mio sire!
No, non piango!
Ma come son, rimango,
che l'oro non può dare
la felicità!"
MAGDA: Perchè non continuate?
PRUNIER: Il seguito mi manca:

se voi l'indovinate
vi cedo la mia gloria.
MAGDA: La conquista mi tenta,
e la semplice istoria!
Chi il bel sogno di Doretta
potè indovinar?
Il suo mistero come mai finì?
Ahimè! un giorno uno studente
in bocca la baciò
e fu quel bacio
rivelazione:
fu la passione! . . .
Folle amore!
Folle ebbrezza!
Chi la sottile carezza
d'un bacio sì ardente
mai ridir potrà?
TUTTI: Deliziosa!

PRUNIER: Who was able to guess
Doretta's beautiful dream?
No one ever discovered her secret!
One fine day the king wanted
to get to know the girl:
"If you trust me,
if you yield to me,
I'll make you rich!
Ah! child!
Sweet enchantment!
Your futile fear,
your warm tears
will now disappear!"
"No, my lord!
No, I am not weeping!
But as I am, I remain,
for gold cannot give
happiness!"
MAGDA: Why don't you go on?
PRUNIER: I'm at a loss for the continuation:

if you come up with it
I'll surrender my glory to you.
MAGDA: The conquest tempts me,
and the simple story!
Who was able to guess
Doretta's beautiful dream?
How did her secret turn out?
Alas! One day a student
kissed her on the lips
and that kiss was
a revelation:
it was passion! . . .
Mad love!
mad intoxication!
Who can ever describe
the subtle caress
of such an ardent kiss?
TUTTI: She's charming!

*Usually recorded in recitals merely as a soprano performance; the whole number is given here for completeness and clarity.

MAGDA: Ah! mio sogno!
Ah! . . . mia vita! . . .
TUTTI: È squisita! È squisita!
MAGDA: Che importa la ricchezza
se alfine è rifiorita
la felicità! . . .

MAGDA: Ah! my dream!
Ah! . . . my life! . . .
TUTTI: She's superb! She's superb!
MAGDA: What's the good of riches
when happiness
has finally blossomed again! . . .

SUOR ANGELICA

(1918; libretto by Giovacchino Forzano, 1884–1970)

Senza mamma (Suor Angelica)

Senza mamma, o bimbo, tu sei morto!
Le tue labbra, senza i baci miei,
scoloriron fredde, fredde!
E chiudesti, o bimbo, gli occhi belli.

You died far from your mother, my baby!
Without my kisses, your lips
grew pale and cold!
And you closed your beautiful eyes, my baby.

Non potendo carezzarmi,
le manine componesti in croce!
E tu sei morto senza sapere
quanto t'amava questa tua mamma!

Unable to caress me,
you crossed your little hands!
And you died without knowing
how much this mother of yours loved you!

Ora sei un angelo del cielo,
ora tu puoi vederla, la tua mamma,
tu puoi scendere giù pel firmamento
ed aleggiare intorno a me ti sento.

Now you're an angel in heaven,
now you can see her, your mother,
you can come down through the skies
and I feel you hovering around me.

Sei qui, sei qui, mi baci e mi accarezzi.
Ah! Dimmi, quando in ciel potrò vederti?
Quando potrò baciarti?
O dolce fine d'ogni mio dolore,
quando in cielo con te potrò salire?

You're here, you're here, you kiss me and caress me.
Ah! Tell me, when can I see you in heaven?
When can I kiss you?
Oh sweet finale to all my sorrow,
when can I ascend to heaven with you?

Quando potrò morire?
Dillo alla mamma, creatura bella,
con un leggiero scintillar di stella,
parlami, parlami, amore, amore, amor!

When can I die?
Tell your mother, beautiful child,
with the slight twinkling of a star,
speak to me, speak to me, love, love, love!

GIANNI SCHICCHI

(1918; libretto by Giovacchino Forzano, 1884–1970)

O mio babbino caro (Lauretta)

O mio babbino caro,	O my dearest daddy,
mi piace, è bello, bello,	I love him, he's handsome, handsome,
vo' andare in Porta Rossa	I want to go to the Porta Rossa [Red Gate]
a comperar l'anello!	to buy the ring!
Sì, sì, ci voglio andare!	Yes, yes, I want to go there!
E se l'amassi indarno	And if my love for him should be in vain,
andrei sul Ponte Vecchio	I'd go to the Ponte Vecchio
ma per buttarmi in Arno!	but in order to throw myself into the Arno!
Mi struggo e mi tormento,	I'm pining and I'm suffering,
O Dio! Vorrei morir!	O God! I'd like to die!
Babbo, pietà, pietà!	Daddy, have pity, have pity!

Gioacchino Rossini (1792–1868)

TANCREDI *(1813; libretto by Gaetano Rossi, 1774–1855)*

Di tanti palpiti (Tancredi, ACT I)

Oh patria! dolce e ingrata patria!	O homeland! Sweet and thankless homeland!
alfine a te ritorno!	At last I return to you!
Io ti saluto, o cara terra	I greet you, o dear land
degli avi miei: ti bacio.	of my ancestors: I kiss you.
È questo per me giorno sereno,	For me this is a peaceful day,
comincia il core a respirarmi in seno.	the heart in my breast begins to beat anew.
Amenaide! o mio pensier soave,	Amenaide! O my sweet thought,
solo de' miei sospiri,	the sole heavenly object
de' voti miei celeste oggetto!	of my sighs, of my vows!
Io venni alfin: io voglio,	I've come at last: I wish—
sfidando il mio destino,	in defiance of my fate,
qualunque sia, meritarti,	whatever it may be—to deserve you
o perire, anima mia.	or die, my soul.
Tu che accendi questo core,	You who set this heart on fire,

tu che desti il valor mio,	you who arouse my daring,
alma gloria, dolce amore,	divine glory, sweet love,
secondate il bel desio;	aid my wonderful wish;
cada un empio traditore,	let a wicked traitor fall,
coronate il mio valor.	reward my bravery.
Di tanti palpiti, di tante pene,	For so much heartache, so much pain,
da te mio bene, spero mercè.	I hope for recompense from you, my dear.
Mi rivedrai . . .	You will see me again . . .
ti rivedrò . . .	I shall see you again . . .
ti rivedrò . . .	I shall see you again . . .
ne' tuoi bei rai mi pascerò.	I shall be sustained by your beautiful eyes.
Oh, cari momenti,	Oh, precious moments,
oh, dolci contenti (etc.).	oh, sweet contentment (etc.).
Sarà felice, il cor mel dice,	My heart tells me my fate
il mio destino vicino a te.	will be a happy one at your side.
Mi rivedrai . . .	You will see me again . . .
ti rivedrò . . .	I shall see you again . . .
ti rivedrò . . .	I shall see you again . . .
ne' tuoi bei rai mi pascerò,	I shall be sustained by your beautiful eyes.
mi rivedrai . . .	You will see me again . . .
ti rivedrò (etc.).	I shall see you again (etc.).

L'ITALIANA IN ALGIERI
(1813; libretto by Angelo Anelli, 1761–1820)

Cruda sorte (Isabella, ACT I)

Cruda sorte! Amor tiranno!	Cruel fate! Tyrant love!
Questo è il premio di mia fè?	Is this the reward for my fidelity?
Non v'è orror, terror, nè affanno	There's no horror, fear nor anxiety
pari a quel ch'io provo in me.	like those I experience within me.
Per te solo, o mio Lindoro,	For you alone, o my Lindoro,
io mi trovo in tal periglio.	do I find myself in such danger.
Da chi spero, O Dio! consiglio?	From whom am I to hope for advice, o God?
Chi conforto mi darà?	Who will comfort me?
[a few words for Chorus]	[a few words for Chorus]
Qua ci vuol disinvoltura,	This will need coolheadedness,
non più smanie, nè paura;	no more rage nor fear;
di coraggio è tempo adesso.	now it's time to be brave.
Or chi sono si vedrà.	Now we'll see what I'm made of.

Già so per pratica	I already know from experience
qual sia l'effetto	the effect
d'un guardo languido,	of a languishing glance,
d'un sospiretto . . .	of a little sigh . . .
So a domar gli uomini	I know how taming the men
come si fa.	is done.
Sien dolci, o ruvidi,	Be they gentle or rude,
sien flemma, o foco,	be they stodgy or fiery,
son tutti simili	they're all the same
a presso a poco . . .	very nearly . . .
Tutti la chiedono,	They all ask for it,
tutti la bramano,	they all hanker after it,
da vaga femmina	happiness
felicità.	with a pretty woman.

IL BARBIERE DI SIVIGLIA

(1816; libretto by Cesare Sterbini, 1784–1831)

Ecco ridente (Almaviva, ACT I)

Ecco ridente in cielo	Behold, smiling in the sky
spunta la bella aurora,	the lovely dawn is breaking,
e tu non sorgi ancora,	and you do not yet arise
e puoi dormir così?	and can sleep on like this?
Sorgi, mia dolce speme,	Arise, my sweet hope,
vieni, bell'idol mio,	come, my lovely adored one,
rendi men crudo, oh Dio!	make less painful, oh Lord!
lo stral che mi ferì.	the arrow that pierced me.
Oh sorte! già veggo	Oh, fate! I already see
quel caro sembiante;	that dear face;
quest'anima amante	this loving soul
ottenne pietà.	has obtained mercy.
Oh istante d'amore!	Oh, moment of love!
Felice momento!	Happy moment!
Oh dolce contento!	Oh, sweet contentment
che eguale non ha!	that has no equal!

Largo al factotum (Figaro, ACT I)

La ran la le ra,	La ran la le ra,
la ran la la.	la ran la la.
Largo al factotum	Make way for the city's
della città.	jack-of-all-trades.
Presto, a bottega,	Quick, to the shop,
chè l'alba è già!	for it's already dawn!

Ah, che bel vivere,
che bel piacere,
per un barbiere
di qualità!
Ah bravo Figaro!
Bravo, bravissimo!
Fortunatissimo,
per verità! (etc.)
Pronto a far tutto
la notte e il giorno,
sempre d'intorno,
in giro sta.
Miglior cuccagna
per un barbiere,
vita più nobile
no, non si dà.
Rasori e pettini,
lancette e forbici,
al mio comando
tutto qui sta. (etc.)
V'è la risorsa
poi del mestiere
con la donnetta,
col cavaliere . . . (etc.)
Ah che bel vivere,
che bel piacere
per un barbiere
di qualità!
Tutti mi chiedono,
tutti mi vogliono:
donne, ragazzi,
vecchi, fanciulle.
Qua la parrucca . . .
Presto la barba!
Qua la sanguigna . . .
Presto, il biglietto! (etc.)
Figaro! Figaro!
Ahimè, che furia!
Ahimè, che follia!
Uno alla volta,
per carità! (etc.)
Figaro . . . Son qua!
Ehi, Figaro! Son qua!
Figaro qua . . . Figaro là . . .
Figaro su . . . Figaro giù . . .
Pronto, prontissimo!
Son come il fulmine!

Ah, what a lovely life,
what great good times
for a first-rate
barber!
Ah! gallant Figaro!
Bravo, bravissimo!
A most fortunate man
indeed! (etc.)
Ready to do anything
by night and by day,
always present,
he makes the rounds.
Greater good fortune
for a barber,
a more illustrious life
doesn't exist, no.
Razors and combs,
lancets and scissors
all await
my orders here. (etc.)
Then, there are the resources
of my profession
with the ladies,
with the gentlemen . . . (etc.)
Ah, what a lovely life,
what great good times
for a first-rate
barber!
Everyone asks for me,
everyone wants me:
ladies, boys,
old men, girls.
The wig over here . . .
Quick, a shave!
A bloodletting over here . . .
Quick, a message! (etc.)
Figaro! Figaro!
Alas, what frenzy!
Alas, what madness!
One at a time,
for pity's sake! (etc.)
Figaro . . . I'm here!
Hey, Figaro! I'm here!
Figaro here . . . Figaro there . . .
Figaro up . . . Figaro down . . .
I'm coming, I'm coming right away!
I'll be there in a flash!

Sono il factotum	I'm the city's
della città!	jack-of-all-trades!
Ah, bravo Figaro!	Ah, gallant Figaro!
Bravo, bravissimo! (etc.)	Bravo, bravissimo! (etc.)
A te fortuna non mancherà! (etc.)	You will never want for good luck! (etc.)

Una voce poco fa (Rosina, ACT I)

Una voce poco fa	A little while ago a voice
qui nel cor mi risuonò;	echoed here in my heart;
il mio cor ferito è già,	my heart is already stricken,
e Lindor fu che il piagò.	and it was Lindoro who wounded it.
Sì, Lindoro mio sarà;	Yes, Lindoro will be mine;
lo giurai, la vincerò.	I've sworn it, I'll win out.
Il tutor ricuserà,	My guardian will refuse,
io l'ingegno aguzzerò.	I'll sharpen my wits.
Alla fin si accheterà	finally he'll calm down
e contenta io resterò . . .	and I'll be satisfied . . .
Sì, Lindoro mio sarà;	Yes, Lindoro will be mine;
lo giurai, la vincerò.	I've sworn it, I'll win out.
Io sono docile, son rispettosa,	I'm docile, I'm respectful,
sono obbediente, dolce, amorosa;	I'm obedient, sweet, loving;
mi lascio reggere, mi fo guidar.	I let myself be ruled, I allow myself to be guided.
Ma se mi toccano dov'è il mio debole,	But if they touch me on my sore spot,
sarò una vipera e cento trappole	I'll be a viper and I'll devise
prima di cedere farò giocar. (etc.)	a hundred snares before I give up. (etc.)

La calunnia (Basilio, ACT I)

La calunnia è un venticello,	Slander is a little breeze,
un'auretta assai gentile	a very gentle little puff of air
che insensibile, sottile,	that imperceptibly, softly,
leggermente, dolcemente,	lightly, sweetly
incomincia a sussurrar.	begins to whisper.
Piano piano, terra terra,	Soft, soft, low, low,
sotto voce, sibilando,	whispering in an undertone,
va scorrendo, va ronzando;	it goes gliding, it goes buzzing;
nelle orecchie della gente	adroitly it slips
s'introduce destramente,	into people's ears,
e le teste ed i cervelli	it begins to numb and swell up
fa stordire e fa gonfiar.	their heads and brains.
Dalla bocca fuori uscendo	Issuing from their mouths,
lo schiamazzo va crescendo,	the noise goes on increasing,

prende forza poco a poco,
vola già di loco in loco;
sembra il tuono, la tempesta,
che nel sen de la foresta
va fischiando, brontolando
e ti fa d'orror gelar.
Alla fin trabocca e scoppia,
si propaga, si raddoppia
e produce un'esplosione
come un colpo di cannone,
un tremuoto, un temporale,
un tumulto generale,
che fa l'aria rimbombar.
E il meschino calunniato,
avvilito, calpestato,
sotto il publico flagello
per gran sorte va a crepar.

little by little it gathers strength,
soon it flies from place to place;
it's like thunder, a storm
that in the heart of the forest
goes whistling and roaring
and makes you freeze with fright.
Finally it overflows and bursts,
it spreads, it multiplies
and causes an explosion
like a cannon shot,
an earthquake, a thunderstorm,
a universal racket
that makes the air ring.
And the poor slandered wretch,
vilified, trampled on,
scourged by the public,
has the great good luck to croak.

A un dottor della mia sorte (Bartolo, ACT I)

A un dottor della mia sorte
queste scuse, signorina?
Vi consiglio, mia carina,
un po' meglio a impostur ar. (etc.)
I confetti alla ragazza!
Il ricamo sul tamburo!
Vi scottaste: eh via! eh via!

Ci vuol altro, figlia mia,
per potermi corbellar. (etc.)

Perche manca là quel foglio?

Vo' saper codesto imbroglio.
Sono inutili le smorfie;
Ferma là, non mi toccate!
Figlia mia, non lo sperate,
ch'io mi lasci infinocchiar.
Via, carina, confessate:
son disposto a perdonar.
Non parlate? Vi ostinate?

So ben io quel che ho da far.
Signorina, un'altra volta
quando Bartolo andrà fuori,
la consegna ai servitori

To a doctor like me
such fibs, young lady?
I advise you, my dear,
to deceive a little better. (etc.)
Candies to the girl!
Embroidering on a hoop!
You burned yourself! Oh, go on!
    Oh, go on!

It will take more than that, my girl,
to pull the wool over my eyes.
    (etc.)

Why is a sheet of paper missing
    there?

I want to know about this mess.
It's no use making faces;
stop that, don't touch me!
My girl, don't hope
that I'll let you hoodwink me.
Come on, my dear, confess;
I'm in a forgiving mood.
You won't speak? You're being
    stubborn?

Then I know what I have to do.
Young lady, the next time
that Bartolo goes out,
he'll know how to give the servants

a suo modo far saprà.
Ah, non servono le smorfie,
faccia pur la gatta morta.
Cospetton! Per quella porta
nemmen l'aria entrar potrà.

E Rosina, innocentina,
sconsolata, disperata, (etc.)
in sua camera serrata

fin ch'io voglio star dovrà.
Signorina, un'altra volta (etc.).
A un dottor della mia sorte (etc.)?

the proper orders.
Ah, making faces won't work,
go ahead and play the sly one.
By God! not even the air
will be able to come in through
that door!
And little innocent Rosina,
disconsolate, despairing, (etc.)
will have to stay locked up in her
room
just as long as I like.
Young lady, the next time (etc.).
To a doctor like me (etc.)?

LA CENERENTOLA
(1817; libretto by Jacopo Ferretti, 1784–1852)

Non più mesta (Cenerentola, ACT II)

Nacqui all'affanno, al pianto,
soffrì tacendo il core;
ma per soave incanto

dell'età mia nel fiore,
come un baleno rapido
la sorte mia cangiò.
No, no, tergete il ciglio,
perchè tremar, perchè?
A questo sen volate,
figlia, sorella, amica,
tutto trovate in me.
[four lines for other characters]
Padre . . . sposo . . . amico . . . oh,
istante!
Non più mesta accanto al fuoco
sarò sola a gorgheggiar.
Ah, fu un lampo, un sogno, un
giuoco
il mio lungo palpitar.
[CHORUS: Tutto cangia a poco a
poco:
cessa alfin di sospirar.]

I was born to sorrow, to weeping,
my heart suffered silently;
but by means of a delightful magic
spell
in the flower of my years,
quick as a flash,
my fortune changed.
No, no, dry your eyes,
why tremble, why?
Fly to this bosom,
a daughter, sister, friend,
all these you'll find in me.
[four lines for other characters]
Father . . . husband . . . friend . . .
oh, wonderful moment!
No longer will I sing sadly,
alone beside the fire.
Ah, my long heartache

was a flash, a dream, a jest.
[CHORUS: Everything changes little
by little:
cease sighing at last.]

SEMIRAMIDE *(1823; libretto by Gaetano Rossi, 1774–1855)*

Bel raggio lusinghier (Semiramide, ACT I)

Bel raggio lusinghier	A beautiful, enticing ray
di speme, e di piacer	of hope and of pleasure,
alfin per me brillò!	at last has shone for me!
Arsace ritornò,	Arsace has returned,
ah, sì, a me verrà,	ah, yes, he'll come to me;
quest'alma che finor	this soul that hitherto
gemè, tremò, languì,	lamented, quavered, pined,
oh! come respirò!	oh! how it has breathed again!
Ogni mio duol sparì	All my sorrow has vanished
dal cor, dal mio pensier	from my heart, from my thoughts
si dileguò il terror!	fear has faded!
Bel raggio lusinghier (etc.) . . .	A beautiful, enticing ray (etc.) . . .
brillò.	shone for me!
La calma a questo cor	Arsace will restore
[brief passage for Women's Chorus]	[brief passage for Women's Chorus]
Arsace renderà,	tranquility to this heart,
Arsace ritornò,	Arsace has returned,
qui, qui a me verrà.	here, here he will come to me.
[brief passage for Women's Chorus]	[brief passage for Women's Chorus]
Ei verrà, verrà.	He will come, he will come.
Dolce pensiero	Sweet thought
di quell'istante,	of this moment,
a te sorride	my loving heart
l'amante cor.	smiles on you.
Come più caro	How much more precious
dopo il tormento	after my suffering
è il bel momento	is the beautiful moment
di pace e amor,	of peace and love,
è il bel momento di gioia e amor!	is the beautiful moment of joy and
(etc., with Chorus)	love! (etc., with Chorus)

Giuseppe Verdi (1813–1901)

ERNANI (1844; libretto by Francesco Maria Piave, 1810–1876)

Ernani, involami (Elvira, ACT I)

Surta è la notte,
e Silva non ritorna!
Ah! non tornasse ei più . . .
Questo odiato veglio,
che quale immondo spettro
ognor m'insegue
col favellare d'amore,
più sempre Ernani
mi confige in core.
Ernani, Ernani, involami
all'abborrito amplesso.
Fuggiamo, se teco vivere
mi fia d'amore concesso,
per antri e lande inospite

ti seguirà il mio piè.
Un Eden di delizia
saran quegli antri a me.
[10-line Women's Chorus, ending:
Sposa domani in giubilo
te ognun saluterà.]
M'è dolce il voto ingenuo
che il vostro cor mi fa.

Tutto sprezzo, che d'Ernani

non favella a questo core.
Non v'ha gemma che in amore
possa l'odio tramutar.
Vola, o tempo e presto reca,
di mia fuga il lieto istante,
vola, o tempo, al core amante,
è supplizio l'indugiar.
[two lines for Chorus]

Night has fallen,
and Silva isn't back!
Oh! I wish he'd never come back . . .
This old man whom I hate,
who like a foul ghost
pursues me constantly
with words of love,
fixes Ernani more and more
firmly in my heart.
Ernani, Ernani, take me away
from his hated embrace.
Let's run away; if love will allow me
to live with you,
through caverns and barren waste-
     lands
my footsteps will follow you.
Those caverns will be to me
an Eden of delights.
[10-line Women's Chorus, ending:
Everyone will jubilantly
greet you as a bride tomorrow.]
The innocent wish
your heart makes for me is sweet
     to me.
I despise everything that does not
     speak
to my heart of Ernani.
There's no jewel that can
change hatred into love.
Fly, o time, and quickly bring
the happy moment of my escape;
fly, o time, to the loving heart;
delay is torment.
[two lines for Chorus]

LUISA MILLER
(1849; libretto by Salvatore Cammarano, 1801–1852)

Quando le sere al placido (Rodolfo, ACT II)

Oh! Fede negar potessi
agl'occhi miei!
Se cielo e terra,
se mortali ed angeli
attestarmi volesser
ch'ella non è rea, mentite!

io risponder dovrei, tutti mentite.
Son cifre sue!
Tanta perfidia!
Un'alma sì nera! Sì mendace!
Ben la conobbe il padre!
Ma dunque i giuri, le speranze,

la gioia, le lagrime, l'affanno?
Tutto è menzogna, tradimento,
 inganno!
Quando le sere al placido
chiaror d'un ciel stellato
meco figgea nell'etere
lo sguardo innamorato,
e questa mano stringermi
dalla sua man sentia . . .
Ah! Mi tradia! Ah! Mi tradia!

Allor, ch'io muto, estatico
da' labbri suoi pendea,
ed ella in suon angelico,
"Amo, amo te sol," dicea,
tal che sembrò l'empireo
aprirsi all'alma mia!
In suono angelico, "Amo te sol,"
 dicea—
Ah! Mi tradia!

Oh! If I could deny the truth
of what my eyes have seen!
If heaven and earth,
if mortals and angels
were to swear to me
that she is not wickedly false,
 "You're lying!"
I would answer, "you're all lying!"
They are her initials!
Such faithlessness!
So black a soul! So false!
Her father knew her well!
But, in that case: the oaths, the
 hopes,
the happiness, the tears?
Everything is falsehood, treachery,
 deceit!
When, in the evenings, in the calm
glimmering of the starlit sky,
her loving glance
looked with mine into the sky
and I felt my hand
pressed by hers . . .
Ah! She was betraying me! Ah!
 She was betraying me!
Then, as I silently, blissfully
hung on her every word,
and she, in angelic tones,
would say, "I love, love only you,"
so that paradise seemed to be
opening itself to my soul!
In angelic tones she said, "I love
 only you"—
Ah! She was betraying me!

RIGOLETTO
(1851; libretto by Francesco Maria Piave, 1810–1876)

Questa o quella (Duke, ACT I)

Questa o quella per me pari sono	To me this woman or that one are the same as
a quant'altre d'intorno mi vedo;	all the others I see around me;
del mio core l'impero non cedo,	I don't surrender command of my heart
meglio ad una che ad altra beltà.	to one beauty any more than to another.
La costoro avvenenza è qual dono,	Their comeliness is like a gift
di che il fato ne infiora la vita;	with which fortune decorates our life.
s'oggi questa mi torna gradita	If this one finds favor with me today,
forse un altra doman lo sarà.	tomorrow perhaps it will be another.
La costanza, tiranna del core,	Fidelity, despot of the heart,
detestiamo qual morbo crudele;	we hate like a cruel plague;
sol chi vuole si serbi fedele.	Let only those remain faithful who wish to.
Non v'ha amor se non v'è libertà.	There's no love where there's no liberty.
De' mariti il geloso furore,	I scorn the jealous rage of husbands
degli amanti le smanie derido;	and the frenzy of lovers;
anco d'Argo i cent'occhi disfido,	I defy even Argus' hundred eyes
se mi punge una qualche beltà.	If some beauty allures me.

Pari siamo (Rigoletto, ACT II)

Pari siamo! Io la lingua, egli ha il pugnale;	We're equals! I have my tongue, he has his dagger.
l'uomo son io che ride, ei quel che spegne!	I'm the man who mocks, he the one who murders!
Quel vecchio maledivami!	That old man cursed me!
O uomini!—o natura!—	O mankind!—O nature!—
vil scellerato mi faceste voi!	You made me a wicked wretch!
Oh rabbia! esser diforme! esser buffone!	Oh fury! To be deformed! To be a jester!
Non dover, non poter altro che ridere!	Not to be permitted, not to be able to do other than joke!

Il retaggio d'ogni uom m'è tolto, il
  pianto!
Questo padrone mio
giovin, giocondo, sì possente, bello,

sonnecchiando mi dice:
Fa ch'io rida, buffone . . .
forzarmi deggio e farlo! Oh danna-
  zione!
Odio a voi, cortigiani schernitori!
Quanta in mordervi ho gioia!
Se iniquo son, per cagion vostra è
  solo.
Ma in altr'uomo qui mi cangio!

Quel vecchio maledivami . . . Tal
  pensiero
perchè conturba ognor la mente
  mia?
Mi coglierà sventura? Ah no, è
  follia!

Every man's legacy is forbidden to
  me: weeping!
This master of mine,
youthful, gay, so powerful, hand-
  some,
as he dozes off tells me:
"Make me laugh, clown" . . .
And I must force myself to do it!
  Oh, damnation!
I hate you, jeering courtiers!
How much I enjoy needling you!
If I'm wicked, it's only because of
  you.
But here I transform myself into
  another man!

That old man cursed me . . . Why
  is that thought
constantly disturbing my mind?

Will misfortune befall me? Ah, no,
  that's madness!

Caro nome (Gilda, ACT II)

Gualtier Maldè! nome di lui sì
  amato,
ti scolpisci nel core innamorato!

Caro nome che il mio cor
festi primo palpitar,
le delizie dell'amor
mi dêi sempre rammentar!
Col pensiero il mio desir

A te sempre volerà,
e fin l'ultimo sospir,
caro nome, tuo sarà.

Gualtier Maldè! name of him so
  beloved,
you are engraved in my adoring
  heart!
Precious name, the first
that caused my heart to throb,
you'll remind me always
of love's delights!
Along with my thoughts my
  longing
will ever fly to you,
and until my dying breath,
precious name, they'll be of you.

Parmi veder le lagrime (Duke, ACT III)

Ella mi fu rapita!
E quando, o ciel? ne' brevi istanti,

prima che il mio presagio interno
sull'orma corsa ancora mi spin-
  gesse!

She was stolen from me!
And when, o heavens? In the brief
  moments
before my inner foreboding
urged me back over the route I had
  taken!

Schiuso era l'uscio! e la magion deserta!	The door was open! And the house empty!
E dove ora sarà quell'angiol caro?	And where is that precious angel now?
Colei che prima potè in questo core	She who was the first who could light the flame
destar la fiamma di costanti affetti?	of steadfast love in this heart?
Colei sì pura, al cui modesto sguardo	She so pure, at whose modest glance
quasi spinto a virtù talor mi credo!	I almost believe myself at times inclined toward virtue!
Ella mi fu rapita!	She was stolen from me!
E chi l'ardiva?—ma ne avrò vendetta:	And who dared to do it?—but I'll be avenged!
Lo chiede il pianto della mia diletta.	The tears of my beloved demand it!
Parmi veder le lagrime	I seem to see the tears
scorrenti da quel ciglio,	flowing from those lashes,
quando fra il dubbio e l'ansia	when, between her worry and fear
del subito periglio,	of impending danger,
dell'amor nostro memore	mindful of our love,
il suo Gualtier chiamò.	she called for her Gualtier.
Ned ei potea soccorerti,	And he could not help you,
cara fanciulla amata;	dear beloved maid;
ei che vorria coll'anima	he that with all his soul would
farti quaggiù beata;	give you bliss in this world;
ei che le sfere agl'angeli	he that because of you did not envy
per te non invidiò!	the angels for their heavenly spheres!

Cortigiani (Rigoletto, ACT III)

Cortigiani, vil razza dannata,	Courtiers, you damned vile race,
per qual prezzo vendeste il mio bene?	for how much did you sell my darling?
A voi nulla per l'oro sconviene!	There's nothing you wouldn't do for gold!
Ma mia figlia è impagabil tesor.	But my daughter is a priceless treasure.
La rendete . . . o, se pur disarmata,	Give her back . . . or even without weapons,
questa man per voi fora cruente;	this hand will be stained with your blood;
nulla in terra più l'uomo paventa, se dei figli difende l'onor.	a man fears nothing more on earth when defending his children's honor.

Quella porta, assassini, m'aprite!
Ah! voi tutti a me contro venite!
Ebben—piango . . . Marullo—si-
    gnore,
tu ch'hai l'alma gentil come il core,

dimmi or tu, dove l'hanno nascosta?

È là? Non è vero? Tu taci! ohimè!

Miei signori, perdono, pietate—
al vegliardo la figlia ridate.

Il ridarla a voi nulla ora costa,

tutto al mondo è tal figlia per me.
    (etc.)

Open that door for me, murderers!
Ah! You're all against me!
Well, then—I'll weep . . . Marullo—
    sir,
you whose soul is kind like your
    heart,
you tell me, where have they
    hidden her?
She's there? Isn't it so? You keep
    silent! Oh, woe!
My lords, pardon, have pity—
return an old man's daughter to
    him!
It will cost you nothing to return
    her now;
that daughter is all the world to
    me. (etc.)

La donna è mobile (Duke, ACT IV)

La donna è mobile
qual piuma al vento,
muta d'accento
e di pensiero.
Sempre un'amabile,
leggiadro viso,
in pianto o in riso,
è menzognero.
È sempre misero
chi a lei s'affida,
chi le confida
mal cauto il core!
Pur mai non sentesi
felice appieno,
chi su quel seno
non liba amore! (etc.)

Woman is fickle
as a feather in the breeze,
she changes her words
and her thoughts.
Ever a lovable,
graceful countenance,
weeping or smiling,
it's deceitful.
That man is always wretched
who places faith in her,
who entrusts to her
his heart misguidedly!
Yet that man never feels
thoroughly happy
who doesn't taste love
on that bosom! (etc.)

IL TROVATORE
(1853; libretto by Salvatore Cammarano, 1801–1852)

Tacea la notte placida (Leonora, ACT I)

Tacea la notte placida
e bella in ciel sereno,

The calm night was silent
and, beautiful in the cloudless sky,

la luna il viso argenteo	the moon was showing her silver face,
mostrava lieto e pieno . . .	joyous and full . . .
Quando suonar per l'aere	When sounding through the air
infino allor sì muto,	so silent up to that moment
dolci s'udiro e flebili	were heard the sweet and mournful
gli accordi d'un liuto,	chords of a lute,
e versi melanconici	and a troubador sang
un trovator cantò.	melancholy verses.
Versi di prece ed umile,	Verses of a prayer, and a humble one,
qual d'uom che prega Iddio;	like that of a man who prays to God;
in quella ripeteasi	in it was repeated
un nome . . . il nome mio!	one name . . . my name!
Corsi al veron sollecita.	Eagerly, I ran to the balcony.
Egli era, egli era desso!	It was he, it was none other than he!
Gioia provai che agli angeli	I felt happiness such as is only
solo è provar concesso!	granted to angels to feel!
Al core, al guardo estatico	To my heart, to my ecstatic eyes
la terra un ciel sembrò!	Earth seemed a very heaven!

Stride la vampa (Azucena, ACT II)

Stride la vampa! La folla indomita	The blaze crackles! The unruly crowd
corre al quel fuoco lieta in sembianza:	runs to that fire with a glad countenance:
Urli di gioia d'intorno echeggiano,	Howls of joy echo all around;
cinta di sgherri donna s'avanza!	surrounded by rough guards, the woman advances!
Sinistra splende sui volti orribili	On their terrible faces shines ominously
la tetra fiamma che s'alza al ciel!	the dismal flame that leaps to the sky!
Stride la vampa, giunge la vittima,	The blaze crackles, the victim arrives,
nero vestita, discinta e scalza!	black-clad, disheveled and barefoot!
Grido feroce di morte levasi;	A fearful shriek of death arises;
L'eco il ripete di balza in balza!	its echo resounds from crag to crag!
Sinistra splende sui volti orribili	On their terrible faces shines ominously
la tetra fiamma che s'alza in ciel!	the dismal flame that leaps to the sky!

Il balen del suo sorriso (Count, ACT II)

Il balen del suo sorriso	The flash of her smile
d'una stella vince il raggio!	outdoes the beam from a star!
Il fulgor del suo bel viso	The brightness of her beautiful face
nuovo infonde a me coraggio!	inspires me with fresh daring!
Ah! L'amor, l'amore ond'ardo	Ah! Let the love, the love with which I burn
le favelli in mio favor!	speak to her on my behalf!
Sperda il sole d'un suo sguardo	Let the sunshine of one of her glances
la tempesta del mio cor!	disperse the storm in my heart!

Ah! sì, ben mio (Manrico, ACT III)

Ah! sì, ben mio, coll'essere	Ah! yes, my love, with you
io tuo, tu mia consorte,	as my spouse, and I as yours,
avrò più l'alma intrepida,	my soul will be bolder,
il braccio avrò più forte.	my arm will be stronger.
Ma pur, se nella pagina	And yet, if on the page
de' miei destini è scritto	of my destiny it is written
ch'io resti fra le vittime,	that I shall remain among the fallen,
dal ferro ostil trafitto,	pierced by the enemy's steel,
fra quegli estremi aneliti	during those last breaths
a te il pensier verrà,	my thoughts will go to you,
e solo in ciel precederti	and death will mean to me
la morte a me parrà.	merely arriving in heaven before you.

Di quella pira (Manrico, ACT III)

Di quella pira l'orrendo fuoco	The dreadful fire of that pyre
Tutte le fibre m'arse, avvampò!	flared up, burned my every fiber!
Empii, spegnetela, o ch'io fra poco	Evil ones, extinguish it, or shortly
col sangue vostro la spegnerò.	I shall extinguish it with your blood.
Ero già figlio prima d'amarti,	I was her son before I loved you,
Non può frenarmi il tuo martir!	your suffering cannot restrain me!
Madre infelice, corro a salvarti,	Unlucky mother, I rush to save you,
o teco almeno corro a morir!	or at least I rush to die with you!
[interspersed with lines for Leonora, Ruiz & Men's Chorus]	[interspersed with lines for Leonora, Ruiz & Men's Chorus]

D'amor sull'ali rosee (Leonora, ACT IV)

In questa oscura
notte ravvolta, presso a te son io,
e tu nol sai! Gemente
aura, che intorno spiri,
deh pietosa gli arreca i miei sospiri.

D'amor sull'ali rosee
vanne, sospir dolente,
del prigioniero misero
conforta l'egra mente.
Com'aura di speranza
aleggia in quella stanza;
lo desta alle memorie,
ai sogni dell'amor!
Ma, deh! Non dirgli, improvvido,
le pene del mio cor!

Enveloped
in this dark night, I'm near you,
and you don't know it! Moaning
breeze that blows around me,
pray take pity and carry my sighs
to him.
On the roseate wings of love
go, mournful sigh,
comfort the weary thoughts
of the unhappy prisoner.
Like a breath of hope
flutter to that room;
awaken him to memories,
to dreams of love.
But pray! Do not rashly tell him
of the pain in my heart!

LA TRAVIATA

(1853; libretto by Francesco Maria Piave, 1810–1876)

È strano . . . Ah, fors'è lui . . . Sempre libera (Violetta, ACT I)

È strano! È strano! In core
scolpiti ho quegli accenti!
Saria per mia sventura un serio
   amore?
Che risolvi, o turbata anima mia?

Null'uomo ancora t'accendeva. O
   gioia
ch'io non conobbi, esser amata
   amando!
E sdegnarla poss'io
per l'aride follie del viver mio?

Ah, fors'è lui che l'anima

solinga ne' tumulti,
godea sovente pingere
de' suoi colori occulti!
Lui, che modesto e vigile

Strange! Strange! Those words
are engraved on my heart!
Might it be a serious love, to my
   misfortune?
How will you decide, my confused
   soul?

No man has ever set you aflame! O
   joy
I've never known, to love and be
   loved in return!
And can I disdain it
for the barren follies of my exis-
   tence?

Ah, perhaps this is he whom my
   soul,
lonely amid the uproar,
often delighted to paint
in its secret colors!
He who, unassuming and watchful,

all'egre soglie ascese,

e nuova febbre accese,
destandomi all'amor!
A quell'amor ch'è palpito
dell'universo intero,
misterïoso, altero,
croce e delizia al cor.
A me, fanciulla, un candido
e trepido desire,
quest'effigiò dolcissimo
signor dell'avvenire,
quando ne' cieli il raggio
di sua beltà vedea,
e tutta me pascea
di quel divino error.
Sentia che amore è palpito
dell'universo intero,
misterïoso, altero,
croce e delizia al cor!
Follie! Follie!
Delirio vano è questo!
Povera donna, sola,
abbandonata in questo
popoloso deserto
che appellano Parigi,
che spero or più?
Che far degg'io? Gioire!
Di voluttà ne' vortici,
di voluttà perir!
Gioir! Gioir!
Sempre libera degg'io
folleggiare di gioia in gioia,
vo' che scorra il viver mio
pei sentieri del piacer.
Nasca il giorno o il giorno muoia,

sempre lieta ne' ritrovi

a diletti sempre nuovi
dee volare il mio pensier.
[repetitions, with a little music for
    Alfredo]

came up to the threshold of my
    sickroom,
and kindled a new fever,
awakening me to love!
To that love which is the heartbeat
of the whole universe,
mysterious, proud,
pain and delight to the heart.
When I was a girl, an innocent
and anxious longing
portrayed for me this most gentle
lord of my future,
when I used to see the radiance
of his good looks in the sky
and nourished myself entirely
on those divine imaginings.
I felt that love is the heartbeat
of the whole universe,
mysterious, proud,
pain and delight to the heart!
Madness! Madness!
This is a vain dream!
A poor woman, alone,
forsaken in this
populous wasteland
called Paris,
what hope is there left for me?
What should I do? Enjoy myself!
Perish in a vortex of pleasure,
of pleasure!
Enjoy myself! Enjoy myself!
Forever free, I must
dash madly from joy to joy,
I want my life to run its course
on the pathways of pleasure.
Whether the day is being born or
    the day is dying,
I will be constantly merry at
    gatherings,
my thoughts must soar
to ever fresh delights.
[repetitions, with a little music for
    Alfredo]

De' miei bollenti spiriti (Alfredo, ACT II)

Lunge da lei per me non v'ha diletto!	There's no joy for me away from her!
Volaron già tre lune	Three months have already flown by
dacchè la mia Violetta	since my Violetta
agi per me lasciò, dovizie, amori,	gave up for my sake luxury, wealth, lovers,
e le pompose feste	and the grand parties
ove, agli omaggi avvezza,	where, accustomed to compliments,
vedea schiavo ciascun di sua bellezza.	she saw that every man was a slave to her beauty.
Ed or contenta in questi ameni luoghi	And now, contented in this pleasant place,
tutto scorda per me. Qui presso	she forgets it all for my sake. Here, near
a lei io rinascer mi sento,	her, I feel I'm reborn,
e dal soffio d'amor rigenerato	and, regenerated by the breath of love,
scordo ne' gaudi suoi tutto il passato.	in its pleasures I forget all the past.
De' miei bollenti spiriti	The youthful ardor
il giovanile ardore	of my soaring spirits
ella temprò col placido	she soothed with the calm
sorriso dell'amor!	smile of her love!
Dal dì che disse: Vivere	From the day she said "I want to live
io voglio a te fedel,	faithful to you,"
dell'universo immemore	heedless of the world,
io vivo quasi in ciel.	I've been living almost in paradise.

Di Provenza (Germont, ACT II)

Mio figlio!	My son!
Oh quanto soffri! Oh tergi il pianto,	Oh how you're suffering! Oh, dry your tears,
ritorna di tuo padre orgoglio e vanto.	return to your father as his pride and boast.
Di Provenza il mar, il suol,	Who erased from your heart
chi dal cor ti cancellò?	Provence's sea and soil?
Al natio fulgente sol	What fate snatched you
qual destino ti furò?	from your brilliant native sun?
Oh, rammenta pur nel duol	Oh, even in your sorrow remember
ch'ivi gioia a te brillò,	that joy gleamed for you there,

e che pace colà sol
su te splendere ancor può.
Dio mi guidò!
Ah! il tuo vecchio genitor
tu non sai quanto soffrì.
Te lontano, di squallor
il suo tetto si coprì.
Ma se alfin ti trovo ancor,
se in me speme non fallì,
se la voce dell'onor
in te appien non ammutì,
Dio m'esaudì!

and that only there can peace
still shine on you again.
God has guided me!
Ah! You don't know how much
your old father has suffered.
With you far away, his house
has been steeped in gloom.
But if at last I've found you again,
if my hope hasn't deceived me,
if the voice of honor
isn't completely silenced in you,
God has heard my prayer!

Addio, del passato (Violetta, ACT IV)

"Teneste la promessa—la disfida
ebbe luogo! Il barone fu ferito però
migliora. Alfredo è in stranio suolo;
il vostro sacrificio io stesso gli ho
svelato; egli a voi tornerà pel suo
perdono; io pur verrò. Curatevi—
mertate un avvenir migliore. Giorgio Germont."

"You kept your promise—the
duel took place! The baron was
wounded but is improving. Alfredo
is on foreign soil; I myself revealed
your sacrifice to him; he will come
back to you to ask forgiveness; I
shall come, too. Take care of yourself—you deserve a better future.
Giorgio Germont."

È tardi!
Attendo, attendo—né a me giungon mai!
Oh, come son mutata!
Ma il dottore a sperar pure m'esorta!
Ah, con tal morbo ogni speranza è morta.
Addio, del passato bei sogni ridenti,

le rose del volto già sono pallenti;

l'amore d'Alfredo perfino mi manca,
conforto, sostegno, dell'anima stanca.
Ah! della traviata sorridi al desio,

a lei deh perdona, tu accoglila, o Dio!
Ah! tutto, tutto finì, or tutto, tutto finì!

It's too late!
I wait, I wait—and they never come to me!
Oh, how I've changed!
But the doctor still encourages me to have hope!
Ah, with an illness like this every hope is dead.
Farewell, lovely bright dreams of the past,
the roses in my cheeks are already fading!
Even Alfredo's love is lost to me,
the comfort and support of my weary soul.
Ah! smile on the fallen woman's wish,
pray forgive her, receive her, o Lord!
Ah! Everything, everything is over, now everything, everything is over!

Le gioie, i dolori tra poco avran fine;	Soon joys and sorrows will be at an end;
la tomba ai mortali di tutto è confine!	for mortals the tomb is the outer limit of everything!
Non lacrima o fiore avrà la mia fossa!	My grave will receive neither tears nor flowers!
Non croce col nome che copra quest'ossa!	There will be no cross bearing my name to cover these bones!
Ah! della traviata sorridi al desio,	Ah! smile on the fallen woman's wish,
a lei deh perdona, tu accoglila, o Dio!	pray forgive her, receive her, o Lord!
Ah! tutto, tutto finì, or tutto, tutto finì!	Ah! Everything, everything is over, now everything, everything is over!

I VESPRI SICILIANI

(Les Vêpres Siciliennes; 1855; original French libretto by Eugène Scribe, 1791–1861, and Charles Duveyrier [dates unavailable]; Italian translation by Eugenio Caimi [dates unavailable])

O tu Palermo (Procida, ACT II)

O patria, o cara patria,	O fatherland, O precious fatherland,
alfin, alfin ti veggo!	at last, at last I see you!
L'esule ti saluta	The exile greets you
dopo sì lunga assenza.	after so long an absence.
Il fiorente tuo suolo	Filled with love, I kiss your
ripien d'amore io bacio,	flowering soil,
reco il mio voto a te	I give you my good wishes
col braccio e il core!	with heart and hand!
O tu Palermo, terra adorata,	O Palermo, adored land,
a me sì caro riso d'amor!	so dear a smile of love to me!
Ah! Alza la fronte tanto oltraggiata,	Ah! Lift your head, so greatly outraged,
il tuo ripiglia premier splendor!	resume your former greatness!
Chiesi aita a straniere nazioni,	I sought help from foreign nations,
ramingai per castella e città;	wandering through castles and towns;
ma insensibil al fervido sprone	but heedless of my impassioned goading,
dicea ciascun:	each one said:
Siciliani, ov'è il prisco valor?	"Sicilians, where is your former courage?

Su, sorgete, sorgete a vittoria, all'onor!	Come, rise up, rise up to victory, to honor!"
O tu Palermo (etc.).	O Palermo (etc.).
Il tuo ripiglia almo splendor (etc.).	Resume your divine magnificence (etc.).

Mercè, dilette amiche (Bolero; Elena, ACT V)

Mercè, dilette amiche,	Thank you, beloved friends,
di quei leggiadri fior;	for these pretty flowers;
il caro dono è immagine	the precious gift reflects
del vostro bel candor!	your fine sincerity!
Oh! Fortunato il vincol	Oh! Auspicious the bond
che mi prepara amore,	which love readies for me,
se voi recate pronube	if you, as bridesmaids,
voti felici al core!	bring wishes pleasing to the heart!
Mercè del don!	Thank you for the gift!
O caro sogno, o dolce ebbrezza!	O precious dream, o sweet intoxication!
D'ignoto amor mi balza il cor!	My heart is leaping with unfamiliar love!
Celeste un'aura già respiro,	Already I breathe a heavenly breeze
che tutti i sensi inebbriò.	that has enraptured all my senses.
[brief Chorus of Knights and Maidens]	[brief Chorus of Knights and Maidens]
Oh piagge di Sicilia,	Oh, Sicilian shores,
risplenda un dì seren,	may a peaceful day shine forth;
assai vendette orribili	enough terrible acts of vengeance
ti laceraro il sen!	have wounded your breast!
Di speme colma e immemore	Full of hope and forgetful
di quanto il cor soffrì,	of how much my heart has endured,
il giorno del mio giubilo	may my day of rejoicing
sia di tue glorie il dì.	be a day of glory for you.
Gradisco il don di questi fior,	I accept the gift of these flowers,
ah sì, ah sì!	ah, yes, ah, yes!
O caro sogno, o dolce ebbrezza!	O precious dream, o sweet intoxication!
D'ignoto amor mi balza il cor (etc.). } (WITH CHORUS)	My heart is leaping with unfamiliar love (etc.). } (WITH CHORUS)

SIMON BOCCANEGRA
(1857; libretto by Francesco Maria Piave, 1810–1876)

Il lacerato spirito (Fiesco, PROLOGUE)

A te l'estremo addio, palagio altero,	A last farewell to you, haughty palace,
freddo sepolcro dell'angiolo mio!	my angel's icy tomb!
Nè a proteggerti io valsi! . . . Oh maledetto!	I was helpless to defend you! . . . O accursed man!
E tu, Vergine, soffristi	And you, Virgin, you allowed
rapita a lei la verginal corona?	the ravishing of her maidenly crown?
Ma che dissi! . . . Deliro! . . . Ah, mi perdona!	But what have I said! . . . I'm in delirium! . . . Ah, forgive me!
Il lacerato spirito	The wounded spirit
del mesto genitore	of a wretched father
era serbato a strazio	was reserved for the torture
d'infamia e di dolore.	of shame and sorrow.
Il serto a lei de' martiri	Heaven, full of pity, granted
pietoso il cielo diè . . .	her a martyr's crown . . .
Resa al fulgor degli angeli,	Restored to angelic brightness,
prega, Maria, per me.	Maria, pray for me.

UN BALLO IN MASCHERA
(1859; libretto by Antonio Somma, 1809–1865)

Alla vita (Renato, ACT I)

Alla vita che t'arride	To the life that smiles on you,
di speranze e gaudio piena,	filled with hope and joy,
d'altre mille e mille vite	the fate of a thousand, thousand other lives
il destino s'incatena!	is linked!
Te perduto, ov'è la patria	If you are lost, where is the country
col suo splendido avvenir?	with its shining future?
E sarà dovunque, sempre	And will the passage for wounds
chiuso il varco alle ferite,	remain always barred everywhere
perchè scudo del tuo petto	because the people's affection
è del popolo l'affetto?	is a shield to your breast?
Dell'amor più desto è l'odio	Hatred is more alert than love
le sue vittime a colpir.	to strike its victims.
Te perduto (etc.).	If you are lost (etc.).

Volta la terrea (Oscar, ACT I)

Volta la terrea	She turns her ashen
fronte alle stelle	brow to the stars,
come sfavilla	as her eyes
la sua pupilla,	glitter
quando alle belle	while she predicts
il fin predice	to beautiful ladies the end
mesto o felice	of their love affairs,
dei loro amor!	be it tragic or happy!
È con Lucifero	She's always
d'accordo ognor!	of one mind with Lucifer!
[two lines sung by Riccardo]	[two lines sung by Riccardo]
Chi la profetica	Whoever grabs
sua gonna afferra,	her prophetic skirt,
o passi 'l mare,	whether he goes to sea
voli alla guerra,	or flies to war,
le sue vicende	he learns from that woman
soavi, amare	the events of his future,
da questa apprende	be they sweet or bitter,
nel dubbio cor.	in his doubting heart.
È con Lucifero	She's always
d'accordo ognor!	of one mind with Lucifer!

Re dell'abisso (Ulrica, ACT I)

Re dell'abisso, affrettati,	King of the depths, hasten,
precipita per l'etra,	hurtle through the air,
senza librar la folgore	pierce my rooftop
il tetto mio penetra.	without wielding your lightning.
Omai tre volte l'upupa	Three times already has the hoopoe
dall'alto sospirò;	sighed from on high;
la salamandra ignivora	the fire-eating salamander
tre volte sibilò . . .	has hissed three times . . .
E delle tombe il gemito	And the moaning from the tombs
tre volte a me parlò.	has spoken to me three times.

Ma dall'arido stelo (Amelia, ACT II)

Ecco l'orrido campo ove s'accoppia	Here is the dreadful field where death
al delitto la morte!	is coupled to crime!
Ecco là le colonne . . .	Here is the gallows . . .
La pianta è là, verdeggia al piè.	The plant is there, growing green at its foot.
S'inoltri.	Let me go on.
Ah, mi si aggela il core!	Ah, my heart freezes!

Sino il rumor de' passi miei, qui tutto
m'empie di raccapriccio e di terrore!
E se perir dovessi?
Perire! Ebben, quando la sorte mia,
il mio dover tal è, s'adempia e sia.

Ma dall'arido stello divulsa

come avrò di mia mano quell'erba,
e che dentro la mente convulsa
quell'eterea sembianza morrà,
che ti resta, perduto l'amor,

che ti resta, mio povero cor!

Oh! Chi piange, qual forza m'arretra?
m'attraversa la squallida via?
Su, coraggio . . . e tu fatti di pietra,

non tradirmi, dal pianto ristà;

o finisci di battere e muor,
t'annienta, mio povero cor!
Mezzanotte! Ah, che veggo? Una testa
di sotterra si leva . . . e sospira!

Ha negli occhi il balena dell'ira,
e m'affisa e terribile sta!
Deh! Mi reggi, m'aita, o Signor,
miserere d'un povero cor! (etc.)

Even the sound of my footsteps, everything here
fills me with shuddering and fear!
And what if I should die?
Die! Well, then, when my fate,
my duty is such, let it be accomplished and so be it.

But when I have detached that plant
from its dry stem with my hand,
and within my agitated brain
that heavenly image will die,
what will be left for you, when love is lost,
what will be left for you, my poor heart!

Oh! Who is weeping, what force pulls me back,
blocks my gloomy way?
Come, have courage . . . and turn yourself into stone,
do not betray me, desist from weeping;
or finish your beating and die,
destroy yourself, my poor heart!
Midnight! Ah, what do I see? A head
lifts itself from underground . . . and breathes!
Its eyes flash with anger,
and it stares at me and is terrible!
Pray! Support me, help me, O Lord,
have mercy on an unfortunate heart! (etc.)

Eri tu (Renato, ACT III)

Eri tu che macchiavi quell'anima,
la delizia dell'anima mia;
che m'affidi e d'un tratto esecrabile

l'universo avveleni per me!
Traditor! Che compensi in tal guisa
dell'amico tuo primo la fè!
O dolcezze perdute! O memorie

It was you who sullied that soul,
the delight of my own soul,
you who confide in me and who with one heinous dead
poison the universe for me!
Traitor who repays in such a way
your foremost friend's trust!
O lost delights! O memories

d'un amplesso che l'essere india!

of an embrace that makes one divine!

Quando Amelia, sì bella, sì candida,
sul mio seno brillava d'amor!
È finita, non siede che l'odio
e la morte nel vedovo cor!

When Amelia, so beautiful, so pure,
was radiant with love on my breast!
It's finished, nothing but hatred
and death reside in my widowed heart!

O dolcezze perdute! O speranze d'amor!

Oh lost delights! Oh hopes of love!

Ma se m'è forza perderti (Riccardo, ACT III)

Ma se m'è forza perderti
per sempre, o luce mia,
a te verrà il mio palpito
sotto qual ciel tu sia,

But if I am forced to lose you
forever, o my light,
my heartbeats will come to you
under whichever heaven you may be,

chiusa la tua memoria
nell'intimo del cor,
chiusa nell'intimo del cor.
Ed or qual reo presagio
lo spirito m'assale,
che il rivederti annunzia

the memory of you enclosed
within my inmost heart,
enclosed within my inmost heart.
And now what black foreboding
assails my mind,
which predicts that seeing you again

quasi un desio fatale . . .
Come se fosse l'ultima
ora del nostro amor?
Oh, qual presagio m'assale,
come se fosse l'ultima
ora del nostro amor?

is an almost fatal wish . . .
As if it were the final
hour of our love?
Oh, what foreboding assails me,
as if it were the final
hour of our love?

Saper vorreste (Oscar, ACT III)

Saper vorreste
di che si veste,
quando l'è cosa
ch'ei vuol nascosa.
Oscar lo sa,
ma nol dirà,
tra, la, la, la!
Pieno d'amor
mi balza il cor,
ma pur discreto
serba il secreto.
Nol rapirà

You'd like to know
what he's wearing,
when it's the thing
that he wants to keep secret!
Oscar knows
but he won't say,
tra, la, la, la!
Full of love
my heart is leaping,
and yet discreetly
it keeps the secret.
Neither rank nor beauty

grado o beltà,	will pry it loose,
tra, la, la, la!	tra, la, la, la!
Oscar lo sa,	Oscar knows
ma nol dirà,	but he won't say,
tra, la, la, la!	tra, la, la, la!

LA FORZA DEL DESTINO

(1862; libretto by Francesco Maria Piave, 1810–1876)

Madre, pietosa Vergine (Leonora, ACT II)

Madre, pietosa Vergine,	Mother, Virgin full of pity,
perdona al mio peccato.	forgive my sin.
M'aita quell'ingrato	Help me erase that thankless one
dal core a cancellar.	from my heart.
In queste solitudini	In this lonely place
espierò l'errore . . .	I will atone for my mistakes . . .
Pietà di me, Signore,	Have pity on me, Lord,
Dio, non m'abbandonar.	Do not forsake me, God.

O tu che in seno agli angeli (Alvaro, ACT III)

O tu che in seno agli angeli	O you who ascended, eternally pure,
eternamente pura	beautiful and unscathed,
salisti bella, incolume	from the misfortune of mortals
della mortal iattura,	into the angels' bosom,
non iscordar di volgere	do not forget to turn
lo sguardo a me tapino,	your glance on a wretch like me,
che senza speme ed esule	who, hopeless and in exile,
in odio del destino	hated by destiny,
chiedo anelando, ahi misero,	seeks ardently, alas, unhappy man,
la morte d'incontrar.	to meet death.
Leonora mia, soccorrimi,	My Leonora, help me,
pietà del mio penar.	pity my suffering.

Urna fatale (Carlo, ACT III)

Urna fatale del mio destino,	Fatal choice of my destiny,
va, t'allontana, mi tenti invano;	go away, distance yourself, you tempt me in vain;
l'onor a terger qui venni, e insano	I came here to cleanse my honor, and will not madly
d'un'onta nuova nol macchierò.	soil it with a new shame.

Un giuro è sacro per l'uom d'onore;	An oath is sacred for a man of honor;
que' fogli serbino il lor mistero . . .	let these papers keep their secret . . .
Disperso vada il mal pensiero	May the evil thought vanish
che all'atto indegno mi concitò.	that incited me to an unworthy deed.
E s'altra prova rinvenir potessi?	But if I could find some other proof?
Vediam.	We'll see.
Qui v'ha un ritratto.	There is a portrait here.
Suggel non v'è . . . nulla ei ne disse . . . nulla	There's no seal . . . He said nothing about it . . .
promisi . . . S'apra dunque . . .	I made no promises . . . Then, let me open it . . .
Ciel! Leonora!	Heavens! Leonora!
Don Alvaro è il ferito!	The wounded man is Don Alvaro!
Ora egli viva . . . e di mia man poi muoia . . .	Let him live now . . . and then die at my hands . . .
[CHIRURGO: Lieta novella, è salvo.]	[SURGEON: Good news, he's out of danger.]
È salvo! Oh gioia!	He's out of danger! Oh, joy!
Ah! Egli è salvo! oh gioia immensa	Ah! He's out of danger! Oh, immense joy
che m'innondi il cor, ti sento!	that floods my heart, I feel you!
Potrò alfine il tradimento	At last I will be able to avenge
sull'infame vendicar.	the betrayal on that villain.
Leonora, ove t'ascondi?	Leonora, where are you hiding?
Di': seguisti fra le squadre	Tell me: did you follow among the troops
chi del sangue di tuo padre	the man who made your face turn red
ti fe' il volto rosseggiar?	with your father's blood?
Ah, felice appien sarei	Ah, I would be completely happy
se potesse il brando mio	if my sword could
amendue d'averno al dio	sacrifice both of them with a single blow
d'un sol colpo consacrar!	to the god of the underworld!
Egli è salvo! (etc.)	He's out of danger! (etc.)

Pace, pace, mio Dio! (Leonora, ACT IV)

Pace, pace, mio Dio! Cruda sventura	Peace, peace, my God! Cruel misfortune
m'astringe, ahimè, a languir;	compels me, alas, to pine away;
come il dì primo da tant'anni dura	my suffering has remained for so many years

profondo il mio soffrir.

L'amai, gli è ver! Ma di beltà e valore
cotanto Iddio l'ornò,
che l'amo ancor, nè togliermi dal core
l'immagin sua saprò.
Fatalità! Fatalità! Un delitto
disgiunti n'ha quaggiù! . . .
Alvaro, io t'amo, e su nel cielo è scritto:
non ti vedrò mai più!
Oh Dio, Dio, fa ch'io muoia; che la calma
può darmi morte sol.
Invan la pace qui sperò quest'alma
In preda a lungo duol.

Misero pane . . . a prolungarmi vieni
la sconsolata vita . . . ma chi giunge?
Chi profanare ardisce il sacro loco?

Maledizione! . . . Maledizione! . . .

as deep as on the first day.

I loved him, it's true! But God graced him
with so much beauty and valor
that I love him still and don't know how to tear
his image from my heart.
Destiny! Destiny! A crime
has parted us in this world! . . .
Alvaro, I love you, and it is written in heaven above:
I shall never again see you!
Oh, God, God, let me die;

for only death can give me peace.
In vain has this soul, a prey
to long suffering, hoped for peace here.

Wretched loaf . . . you are here to prolong
my despairing life . . . but who is coming?
Who dares to profane this holy place?

Curses! . . . Curses! . . .

DON CARLO

(Don Carlos; 1867 & 1884; original French libretto by François-Joseph Méry, 1797–1865, and Camille du Locle, 1832–1903; Italian translation by A. de Lauzières and A. Zanardini [dates unavailable])

Ella giammai m'amò (Filippo, ACT IV)

Ella giammai m'amò! No, quel cor chiuso è a me,
amor per me non ha!
Io la rivedo ancor contemplar triste in volto
il mio crin bianco il dì che qui di Francia venne.
No, amor per me non ha,
amor per me non ha!
Ove son? Quei doppier

She never loved me! No, that heart is closed to me,
she has no love for me!
I still see her, looking with a sad face
at my white hair on the day she came here from France.
No, she has no love for me,
she has no love for me!
Where am I? Those candles

presso a finir! L'aurora imbianca il
mio veron!
Già spunta il dì! Passar veggo i miei
giorni lenti!
Il sonno, o Dio! sparì dai miei occhi
languenti!
Dormirò sol nel manto mio regal
quando la mia giornata è giunta a
sera,
dormirò sol sotto la volta nera,

là, nell'avello dell'Escurial.
Se il serto regal a me desse il poter

di leggere nei cor, che Dio può sol
veder!
Se dorme il prence, veglia il traditore;
il serto perde il re, il consorte
l'onore!
Dormirò (etc.).
Ah, se il serto (etc.).
Ella giammai m'amò! No! Quel cor
chiuso è a me,
amor per me non ha!

are almost burned out! The dawn
whitens my balcony!
Already the day is dawning! I see
my idle days passing by!
Sleep, o God! has vanished from
my tired eyes!
I shall sleep alone in my royal robes
when my day has arrived at
evening,
I shall sleep alone under the black
vault,
there, in my tomb in the Escurial.
If my royal crown only gave me
the power
to read hearts that God alone can
see!
When the prince sleeps, the traitor
is vigilant;
the king loses his crown, the husband his honor!
I shall sleep (etc.).
Ah, if my royal crown (etc.).
She never loved me! No! That
heart is closed to me,
she has no love for me!

O don fatale (Eboli, ACT IV)

Ah! Più non vedrò la Regina!
O don fatale, o don crudel
che in suo furor mi fece il cielo!

Tu che ci fai sì vane, altere,

ti maledico, o mia beltà!
Versar, versar sol posso il pianto,

speme non ho, soffrir dovrò!

Il mio delitto è orribil tanto
che cancellar mai nol potrò!
Ti maledico, ti maledico, o mia
beltà!
O, mia Regina, io t'immolai
al folle error di questo cor.

Ah! I'll never see the queen again!
O fatal gift, o cruel gift,
which heaven granted me in its
anger!
You who make us women so vain
and proud,
I curse you, o my beauty!
I can but pour out, pour out my
tears,
I have no hope, I shall have to
suffer!
So horrible is my offense
that I will never be able to erase it!
I curse you, I curse you, o my
beauty!
O my queen, I have sacrificed you
to my heart's insane wrongdoing.

Solo in un chiostro al mondo ormai	Henceforth I shall have to hide my sorrow
dovrò celar il mio dolor!	from the world only in a cloister.
Oh ciel! E Carlo a morte domani,	Oh, heaven! And I shall see Carlo going to his death tomorrow,
gran Dio! a morte andar vedrò!	great God! going to his death!
Ah! Un dì mi resta, la speme m'arride,	Ah! One day remains to me, hope smiles on me,
sia benedetto il ciel! Lo salverò!	blessed be heaven! I will save him!

Per me giunto (Rodrigo, ACT IV)

Per me giunto è il dì supremo,	The last day has arrived for me;
no, mai più ci rivedrem;	no, we'll never see each other again;
ci congiunga Iddio nel ciel,	may God unite us in heaven,
Ei che premia i suoi fedel.	He that rewards those with faith in Him.
Sul tuo ciglio il pianto io miro:	I see tears in your eyes:
lagrimar così, perchè?	Why do you cry thus?
No, fa cor, l'estremo spiro	No, take heart, the final breath
lieto è a chi morrà per te.	of him who will die for you is a joyful one.

O Carlo, ascolta (Rodrigo, ACT IV)

O Carlo, ascolta, la madre t'aspetta	O Carlo, listen, your mother expects you
a San Giusto doman; tutto ella sa . . .	at San Giusto tomorrow; she knows everything . . .
Ah! La terra mi manca . . . Carlo mio,	Ah! I am unsteady on my feet . . . my Carlo,
a me porgi la man!	give me your hand!
Io morrò, ma lieto in core,	I will die, but with a joyful heart,
chè potei così serbar	because I could thus keep safe
alla Spagna un salvatore!	a savior for Spain!
Ah! Di me non ti scordar!	Ah! Do not forget me!
Di me non ti scordar!	Do not forget me!
Sì, regnare tu dovevi,	Yes, you must rule,
ed io morir per te.	and I must die for you.
Ah! Io morrò (etc.) . . . scordar!	Ah! I will die (etc.) . . . forget me!
Ah! La terra	Ah! I am unsteady
mi manca . . . La mano a me . . .	on my feet . . . Your hand to me . . .
Ah! Salva la Fiandra . . .	Ah! Save Flanders . . .
Carlo, addio! Ah! Ah!	Goodbye, Carlo! Ah! Ah!

Tu che le vanità (Elisabetta, ACT V)

Tu che le vanità conoscesti del mondo,
e godi nell'avel il riposo profondo,

se ancor si piange in cielo, piangi sul mio dolore,
e porta il pianto mio al trono del Signor.
Carlo qui verrà, sì! Che parta e scordi omai . . .
A Posa di vegliar sui giorni suoi giurai.
Ei segua il suo destin, la gloria il traccerà.
Per me, la mia giornata a sera è giunta già!
Francia, nobile suol, sì caro a' miei verd'anni!
Fontainebleau! vêr voi schiude il pensier i vanni!
Eterno giuro d'amor là Dio da me ascoltò,
e quest'eternità un giorno sol durò.

Tra voi, vaghi giardin di questa terra ibera,
se Carlo ancor dovrà fermar i passi a sera,
che le zolle, i ruscelli, i fonti, i boschi, i fior,
con le lor armonie cantino il nostro amor.
Addio, bei sogni d'or, illusion perduta!
Il nodo si spezzò, la luce è fatta muta!
Addio, verd'anni ancor! Cedendo al duol crudel,
il cor ha un sol desir: la pace dell'avel!
Tu che le vanità (etc.) . . . trono del Signor.
Se ancor si piange in cielo,
ah, il pianto mio reca a' piè del Signor!

You who know the world's vanities

and who enjoy deep rest in the grave,
if there is yet weeping in heaven, weep for my sorrows,
and carry my tears to the Lord's throne.
Yes, Carlo will come here! Let him now depart and forget . . .
I swore to Posa to watch over his life.
Let him follow his destiny, fame will delineate it.
For me, my day has already reached evening!
France, noble earth, so dear to my young years!
Fontainebleau! My thoughts spread their wings toward you!
There God heard from me a vow of eternal love,
and this eternity lasted only one day.

If Carlo must again walk across you at evening,
delightful gardens of this Spanish land,
let the earth, the brooks, the fountains, the trees, the flowers
sing in concord of our love.

Farewell, beautiful golden dreams, lost illusion!
The knot is broken, the light has been dimmed!
Farewell again, green years! Yielding to cruel sorrow,
my heart has only one wish: the peace of the grave!
You who know the world's vanities (etc.) . . . the Lord's throne.
If there is yet weeping in heaven,
ah, bring my tears to the Lord's feet!

AIDA *(1871; libretto by Antonio Ghislanzoni, 1824–1893)*

Celeste Aida (Radames, ACT I)

Se quel guerrier io fossi!	If only I were that warrior!
Se il mio sogno si avverasse!	If my dream came true!
Un esercito di prodi da me guidato,	An army of brave men led by me,
e la vittoria, e il plauso di Menfi tutta!	and victory, and the plaudits of all of Memphis!
e a te, mia dolce Aida,	and to return to you, my sweet Aida,
tornar di lauri cinto . . .	wreathed in laurels . . .
dirti, "Per te ho pugnato, per te ho vinto!"	to say to you, "I fought for your sake, I conquered for your sake!"
Celeste Aida, forma divina,	Heavenly Aida, divine form,
mistico serto di luce e fior,	mystic garland of light and blossom,
del mio pensiero tu sei regina,	you are the queen of my thoughts,
tu di mia vita sei lo splendor.	you are the glory of my life.
Il tuo bel cielo vorrei ridarti,	I would like to restore to you your lovely sky,
le dolci brezze del patria suol;	the soft breezes of your native land;
un regal serto sul crin posarti,	to place a royal wreath on your locks,
ergerti un trono vicino al sol, ah!	to raise a throne for you beside the sun, ah!
Celeste Aida, forma divina,	Heavenly Aida, divine form,
mistico raggio di luce e fior,	mystic ray of light and blossom,
del mio pensiero tu sei regina (etc.) . . . sol!	you are the queen of my thoughts (etc.) . . . the sun!

Ritorna vincitor (Aida, ACT I)

Ritorna vincitor! E dal mio labbro	May he return as the conqueror! And from my lips
uscì l'empia parola! Vincitor	those wicked words issued! Conqueror
del padre mio, di lui che impugna l'armi	of my father, of the man who brandishes weapons
per me, per ridonarmi	on my behalf, to give me back
una patria, una reggia, e il nome illustre	a homeland, a palace, and the distinguished name
che qui celar m'è forza! Vincitor	that I must keep secret here! Conqueror

de' miei fratelli . . . ond'io lo vegga,
tinto
del sangue amato, trionfar nel
plauso
dell'Egizie coorti! E dietro il carro,

un Re, mio padre, di catene avvinto!

L'insana parola,
o Numi, sperdete!
Al seno d'un padre
la figlia rendete;
struggete le squadre
dei nostri oppressor! Ah!
Sventurata! Che dissi? E l'amor
mio?
Dunque scordar poss'io
questo fervido amore
che, oppressa e schiava,

come raggio di sol qui mi beava?

Imprecherò la morte
a Radames, a lui ch'amo pur tanto!

Ah! Non fu in terra mai
da più crudeli angoscie un core
affranto!
I sacri nomi di padre, d'amante
nè profferir poss'io, nè ricordar;
per l'un, per l'altro confusa e tre-
mante
io piangere vorrei, vorrei pregar.
Ma la mia prece in bestemmia si
muta . . .
delitto è il pianto a me, colpa il
sospir . . .
in notte cupa la mente è perduta,

e nell'ansia crudel vorrei morir.

Numi, pietà del mio soffrir!
Speme non v'ha pel mio dolor.
Amor fatal, tremendo amor,
spezzami il cor, fammi morir!
Numi (etc.).

of my brothers . . . so that I may
see him, stained
with the blood of my loved ones,
victorious among the praises
of the Egyptian troops! And behind
his chariot,
a king, my father, wrapped in
chains!
Oh gods, make
the mad word vanish!
Restore a daughter
to her father's breast;
destroy the armies
of our oppressors! Ah!
Wretched woman! What did I say?
And my beloved?
Can I then forget
that ardent love
which, in my oppression and servi-
tude,
has made me blissful here like a
sunbeam?
Shall I pray for death
to Radames, to the man whom I
after all love so much!
Ah! never on earth was there
a heart crushed by more grievous
sorrows!
I may neither speak nor recollect
the holy names of father, of lover;
confused and quaking, for both
the one and the other
I would weep, I would pray.
But my prayer is turned into
blasphemy . . .
For me, weeping is a crime, sighing
is an offense . . .
my thoughts are lost in gloomy
night,
and in my cruel torment I want to
die.
Gods, pity my suffering!
There's no hope for my sorrow.
Fateful love, tremendous love,
break my heart, make me die!
Gods (etc.).

Oh patria mia (Aida, ACT III)

Qui Radames verrà! Che vorrà dirmi?	Radames will come here! What will he have to tell me?
Io tremo. Ah! se tu vieni a recarmi, o crudel, l'ultimo addio,	I tremble. Ah! if you are coming to wish me a last farewell, cruel one,
del Nilo i cupi vortici.	the dark whirlpools of the Nile
mi daran tomba, e pace forse, e oblìo.	will grant me a grave, and peace perhaps, and oblivion.
Oh patria mia, mai più ti rivedrò! (etc.)	Oh my homeland, I'll never see you again! (etc.)
O cieli azzurri, o dolci aure native,	O azure skies, o sweet native breezes,
dove sereno il mio mattin brillò,	where my tranquil dawn shone . . .
o verdi colli, o profumate rive,	o green hills, o perfumed shores,
o patria mia, mai più ti rivedrò! (etc.)	o my homeland, I'll never see you again! (etc.)
O fresche valli, o queto asil beato	O cool valleys, o peaceful, blessed calm
che un dì promesso dall'amor mi fu;	that was once assured me by my love;
or che d'amore il sogno è dileguato,	now that love's dream has faded,
o patria mia, non ti vedrò mai più! (etc.)	o my homeland, I'll never see you again! (etc.)

OTELLO *(1887; libretto by Arrigo Boito, 1842–1918)*

Esultate (Otello, ACT I)

Esultate! L'orgoglio musulmano sepolto è in mar, nostra e del cielo è gloria!	Rejoice! Muslim pride is entombed in the sea, the glory is ours and heaven's!
Dopo l'armi lo vinse l'uragano.	After our forces, the hurricane vanquished it.

Brindisi: Inaffia l'ugola! (Iago, ACT I)

Inaffia l'ugola!	Wet your gullet!
Trinca, tracanna,	Drink, swallow it down,
prima che svampino	before the song and the glass
canto e bicchier!	disappear!
[CASSIO: Questa del pampino	[CASSIO: This true manna
verace manna	of the vine shoot
di vaghe annugola	clouds the mind

nebbie il pensier.]
Chi all'esca ha morso
del ditirambo
spavaldo e strambo
beva con me!
[CHORUS REPEATS WITH ADAPTED
  WORDS]
(Un altro sorso
e brillo egli è.)
[RODRIGO: (Un altro (etc.) . . . egli
  è.)]
Il mondo palpita quand'io son brillo!
Sfido l'ironico Nume e il destin!
[CASSIO: Come un armonico liuto
  oscillo,
la gioia scalpita sul mio cammin!]

Chi all'esca (etc.) . . . beva con me!

[CHORUS REPEATS]
(Un altro [etc.] . . . egli è.) (WITH
  RODRIGO)
Fuggan dal vivido nappo i codardi
  . . .
[CASSIO: In fondo all'anima ciascun
  mi guardi!]
. . . che in cor nascondono frodi [e
  mister].*
[CASSIO: Non temo, non temo il
  ver.]
[NUMEROUS REPEATS]

with charming mists.]
Whoever has bitten the bait
of the dithyramb,
arrogant and odd,
let him drink with me!
[CHORUS REPEATS WITH ADAPTED
  WORDS]
(Another sip
and he's tipsy.)
[RODRIGO: (Another [etc.] . . .
  tipsy.)]
The world throbs when I am tipsy.
I defy a mocking God and my fate!
[CASSIO: I vibrate like a musical lute,

joy paws the ground on my path-
  way!]
Whoever has bitten (etc.) . . . drink
  with me!

[CHORUS REPEATS]
(Another [etc.] . . . tipsy.) (WITH
  RODRIGO)
Let cowards flee from the lively
  goblet . . .
[CASSIO: Let everyone look into
  the bottom of my soul!]
. . . those who hide in their hearts
  deceptions [and secrets].
[CASSIO: I'm not afraid, I'm not
  afraid of the truth.]
[NUMEROUS REPEATS]

*Verdi omitted the words "e mister."

Credo (Iago, ACT II)

Credo in un Dio crudel che m'ha
  creato
simile a se, e che nell'ira io nomo.

Dalla viltà d'un germe o d'un atomo

vile son nato.
Son scellerato
perchè son uomo

I believe in a cruel God who fash-
  ioned me
like to himself, and whom I name
  in anger.
Out of the vileness of a seed or an
  atom
I was born vile.
I am a villain
because I am a man

e sento il fango originario in me.

Sì! Questa è la mia fè!
Credo con fermo cuor, siccome
    crede
la vedovella al tempio,
che il mal ch'io penso e che da me
    procede
per mio destino adempio.

Credo che il giusto è un istrion
    beffardo
e nel viso e nel cuor,
che tutto è in lui bugiardo:
lagrima, bacio, sguardo,
sacrificio ed onor.
E credo l'uom gioco d'iniqua sorte

dal germe della culla
al verme dell'avel.
Vien dopo tanta irrision la morte,
e poi? La morte è il nulla,
è vecchia fola il ciel.

and feel the primeval slime in
    myself.
Yes! Such is my faith!
I believe with a firm heart, just as
    firmly as
the young widow in church,
that it is my destiny to fulfill

the evil that I think and that issues
    from me.
I believe the just man is a mocking
    actor
both in his face and in his heart,
that everything in him is a lie:
his tears, kiss, look,
sacrifice and honor.
And I believe man is the plaything
    of an evil fate
from the germ of the cradle
to the worm of the grave.
After all that mockery comes death,
and then? Death is nothingness
and Heaven but a foolish old fable.

Era la notte (Iago, ACT II)

Ardua impresa sarebbe; e qual
    certezza
sognate voi? Quell'immondo fatto

sempre vi sfuggirà. Ma pur se
    guida
è la ragione al vero, una sì forte

congettura riserbo che per poco
alla certezza vi conduce. Udite:

Era la notte, Cassio dormia,
gli stavo accanto.
Con interrotte voci tradia
l'intimo incanto.
Le labbra lente, lente movea,
nell'abbandono
del sogno ardente; e allor dicea,

It would be an arduous task; and
    what certainty
do you imagine you'll achieve?
    That foul act
will always elude you. And yet if
    reason
is a guide to the truth, I still have
    such a strong
conjecture that it will practically
lead you all the way to certainty.
    Listen:
It was at night, Cassio was sleeping,
I lay beside him.
With halting words he betrayed
his innermost obsession.
Slowly, slowly, he moved his lips
in the abandon
of an ardent dream; and then he
    said

con flebil suono:
"Desdemona soave! Il nostro
amor s'asconda.
Cauti vegliamo! L'estasi del ciel

tutto m'innonda."
Seguia più vago l'incubo blando;

con molle angoscia,
l'interna imago quasi baciando,

ei disse poscia:
"Il rio destino impreco
che al Moro ti donò."
E allora il sogno in cieco
letargo si mutò.

in plaintive tones:
"Sweet Desdemona! let our
love be hidden.
Let us be wary! The heavenly
ecstasy
quite overwhelms me!"
The pleasant dream became more
ardent yet;
with tender anxiety,
as if he kissed the image in his
head,
he then said:
"I curse the evil fate
that gave you to the Moor!"
And then the dream was changed
into blind torpor.

Dio! Mi potevi scagliar (Otello, ACT III)

Dio! Mi potevi scagliar tutti i mali

della miseria, della vergogna,
far de' miei baldi trofei trionfali

una maceria, una menzogna,
e avrei portato la croce crudel

d'angoscie e d'onte
con calma fronte
e rassegnato al volere del ciel.
Ma, o pianto, o duol! M'han rapito
il miraggio
dov'io, giulivo, l'anima acqueto.

Spento è quel sol, quel sorriso,
quel raggio
che mi fa vivo, che mi fa lieto!

Tu alfin, Clemenza, pio genio
immortal,
dal roseo riso,
copri il tuo viso
santo coll'orrida larva infernal!

God! You could have hurled upon
me all the afflictions
of misery and of shame,
you could have turned my bold
triumphal trophies
into a ruin and a lie,
and I would have borne the cruel
cross
of anxieties and disgraces
with a calm brow,
resigned to heaven's will.
But, o tears, o sorrow! They have
stolen from me the illusion
in which cheerfully I soothe my
soul.
That sun is extinguished, that
smile, that ray
which gives me life, which gives
me joy.
And finally you, too, Mercy, pious,
deathless spirit
of the rosy smile,
are covering your holy face
with the horrible mask of hell!

Salce (Desdemona, ACT IV)

Mia madre aveva una povera ancella,	My mother used to have a poor maid
innamorata e bella;	who was in love and beautiful;
era il suo nome	her name was
Barbara. Amava	Barbara. She loved
un uom che poi l'abbandonò, cantava	a man who then forsook her, and she used to sing
una canzone: la canzon del Salice.	a song: the Willow Song.
Mi disciogli le chiome . . .	Undo my hair . . .
Io questa sera ho la memoria piena	This evening my memory is full
Di quella cantilena:	of that old song:
"Piangea cantando	"She wept, singing
nell'erma landa,	on the lonely heath,
piangea la mesta.	the sad woman wept.
O salce! Salce! Salce!	O willow! Willow! Willow!
Sedea chinando	She would sit with her head
sul sen la testa!	drooping on her bosom!
O salce! Salce! Salce!	O willow! Willow! Willow!
Cantiamo! cantiamo! Il salce funebre	Let us sing! Let us sing! The mournful willow
sarà la mia ghirlanda."	shall be my garland."
Affrettati; fra poco giunge Otello.	Make haste. Otello is coming soon.
"Scorreano i rivi fra le zolle in fior,	"The brooks ran through the flowering turf,
gemea quel core affranto,	that wounded heart would groan,
e dalle ciglia le sgorgava il cor	and from her eyes her heart poured out
l'amara onda del pianto.	the bitter surge of tears.
O salce! Salce! Salce!	O willow! Willow! Willow!
[Cantiam la nenia blanda.]*	[Let us sing the gentle dirge.]
Cantiamo! cantiamo! Il salce funebre	Let us sing! Let us sing! The mournful willow
sarà la mia ghirlanda.	shall be my garland.
Scendean gli augelli a vol dai rami cupi	The birds came down, flying from their somber branches
verso quel dolce canto.	toward that sweet song.
E gli occhi suoi piangevan tanto, tanto,	And her eyes would weep so much, so much,
da impietosir le rupi."	that the stones were filled with pity."
Riponi quest'anello.	Put back this ring.
Povera Barbara! Solea la storia	Poor Barbara! The story used to
con questo semplice suono finir:	end with this simple sound:

*Verdi omitted this line.

"Egli era nato per la sua gloria,
io per amar . . ."
Ascolta. Odo un lamento.
Taci. Chi batte a quella porta?

[EMILIA: È il vento.]
"Io per amarlo e per morir . . .
Cantiamo! Cantiamo!
Salce! Salce! Salce!"
Emilia, addio. Come m'ardon le
    ciglia!
È presagio di pianto. Buona notte.
Ah! Emilia, Emilia, addio, Emilia,
    addio!

"He was born for his fame,
I was born to love . . ."
Listen. I hear a lament.
Be still. Who's knocking at that
    door?

[EMILIA: It's the wind.]
"I was born to love him and die . . .
Let us sing! Let us sing!
Willow! Willow! Willow!"
Emilia, farewell. How my eyes
    burn!
It foretokens weeping. Good night.
Ah! Emilia, Emilia, farewell, Emilia,
    farewell!

Ave Maria (Desdemona, ACT IV)

Ave Maria, piena di grazia, eletta
fra le spose e le vergini sei tu,
sia benedetto il frutto, o benedetta,
di tue materne viscere, Gesù.
Prega per chi adorando a te si
    prostra,
prega pel peccator, per l'innocente,

e pel debole oppresso e pel possente,

misero anch'esso, tua pietà di-
    mostra.
Prega per chi sotto l'oltraggio piega

la fronte e sotto la malvagia sorte;
per noi tu prega
sempre e nell'ora della morte
    nostra.
Ave! Amen!

Hail Mary, full of grace, blessed
are you among wives and maidens,
blessed, o blessed one, be the fruit
of your womb, Jesus.
Pray for her who prostrates her-
    self before you in worship,
pray for the sinner, for the inno-
    cent,
and for the oppressed weak; and
    for the powerful,
who are also wretched, show your
    pity.
Pray for those whose heads are
    bowed
by affronts and spiteful destiny;
Pray for us
now and in the hour of our death.

Hail! Amen.

Niun mi tema (Otello, ACT IV)

Niun mi tema
s'anco armato mi vede. Ecco la fine

del mio cammin . . . Oh! Gloria!
    Otello fu.

Let no one fear me
if he sees me still armed. Here is
    the end
of my journey . . . Oh! Glory!
    Otello is no more.

E tu . . . come sei pallida! E stanca, e muta, e bella,	And you . . . how pale you are! And weary, and mute, and beautiful,
pia creatura nata sotto maligna stella.	pious creature born under an evil star.
Fredda come la casta tua vita, e in cielo assorta.	Cold as your chaste life, and received in heaven.
Desdemona! Desdemona! Ah! Morta! . . . Morta! . . . Morta!	Desdemona! Desdemona! Ah! Dead! . . . Dead! . . . Dead!
Ho un'arma ancor!	I still have a weapon!
[CASSIO: Ah! ferma! TUTTI: Sciagurato!]	[CASSIO: Ah! stop! TUTTI: Unhappy man!]
Pria di ucciderti . . . sposa . . . ti baciai.	Before I killed you . . . wife . . . I kissed you.
Or morendo . . . nell'ombra . . . in cui mi giacio . . .	Now dying . . . in the shadow . . . in which I lie . . .
un bacio . . . un bacio ancora . . . un altro bacio . . .	a kiss . . . again a kiss . . . another kiss . . .

FALSTAFF *(1893; libretto by Arrigo Boito, 1842–1918)*

L'Onore! Ladri! (Falstaff, ACT I)

L'Onore!	Honor!
Ladri! Voi state ligi all'onor vostro, voi!	Rogues! You stand upon your honor, you!
cloache d'ignominia, quando, non sempre, noi	cesspits of shame, when we cannot always
possiam star ligi al nostro. Io stesso, sì, io, io	stand upon ours. I myself, yes, I, I
devo talor da un lato porre il timor di Dio	must sometimes leave the fear of God on one side
e, per necessità, sviar l'onore, usare	and, out of necessity, sidetrack my honor, must use
stratagemmi ed equivoci, destreggiar, bordeggiare.	stratagems and ambiguities, maneuver and contrive.
E voi, coi vostri cenci e coll'occhiata torta	And you, with your tatters and your wily glances
da gattopardo e i fetidi sghignazzi avete a scorta	like a tiger cat's and your stinking sneers have a large provision
il vostro onor! Che onore?! Che onor? Che onor! Che ciancia!	of honor! What honor?! What honor? What about honor! What rubbish!
Che baia! Può l'onore riempirvi la pancia?	What a joke! Can honor fill your belly?

No. Può l'onor rimettervi uno stinco? Non può.	No. Can honor set a shinbone for you? It cannot.
Nè un piede? No. Nè un dito? No. Nè un capello? No.	Or a foot? No. Or a finger? No. Or a hair? No.
L'onor non è chirurgo. Che è dunque? Una parola.	Honor is no surgeon. What is it, then? A word.
Che c'è in questa parola? C'è dell'aria che vola.	What is there in that word? There's air that wafts away.
Bel costrutto! L'onore lo può sentir chi è morto?	A likely story! Can he who's dead feel honor?
No. Vive sol coi vivi? . . . Neppure: perchè a torto	No. Does it live only in the living? . . . Not even that: because falsely
lo gonfian le lusinghe, lo corrompe l'orgoglio,	flattery puffs it up, pride corrupts it,
l'ammorban le calunnie; e per me non ne voglio!	slanders sicken it; and as for me, I want none of it!
Ma, per tornare a voi, furfanti, ho atteso troppo,	But, to come back to you, scoundrels, I've waited too long,
e vi discaccio. Olà! Lesti! Lesti! al galoppo!	and I discharge you. Hey there! Fast! Fast! At the gallop!
Al galoppo! Il capestro assai bene vi sta.	At the gallop! The halter suits you very well!
Ladri! Via! Via di qua! Via di qua!	Rogues! Away! Away from here! Away from here!

È sogno? O realtà? (Ford, ACT II)

E sogno? O realtà? . . . Due rami enormi	It is a dream? Or reality? . . . Two enormous branches
crescon sulla mia testa.	are sprouting on my head.
È un sogno? Mastro Ford! Mastro Ford! Dormi?	Is it a dream? Master Ford! Master Ford! Are you sleeping?
Svegliati! Su! Ti desta!	Wake up! Up! Rouse yourself!
Tua moglie sgarra e mette in mal assetto	Your wife is errant and is putting in bad condition
l'onor tuo, la tua casa ed il tuo letto!	your honor, your house and your bed!
L'ora è fissata, tramato l'inganno;	The hour is settled, the plot is hatched;
sei gabbato e truffato! . . . E poi diranno	you're swindled and defrauded! . . . And then they'll say
che un marito geloso è un insensato!	that a jealous husband is a fool!
Già dietro a me nomi d'infame conio	Behind my back they're already whistling

fischian passando; mormora lo scherno.
O matrimonio: Inferno!
Donna: Demonio!
Nella lor moglie abbian fede i babbei!
Affiderei
la mia birra a un Tedesco,
tutto il mio desco
a un Olandese lurco,
la mia bottiglia d'acquavita a un Turco,
non mia moglie a se stessa. O laida sorte!
Quella brutta parola in cor mi torna:
Le corna! Bue! Capron! Le fusa torte!
Ah! Le corna! Le corna!
Ma non mi sfuggerai! No! Sozzo, reo,
dannato epicureo!
Prima li accoppio
e poi li colgo. Io scoppio!

Vendicherò l'affronto!
Laudata sempre sia
nel fondo del mio cor la gelosia.

shameful names in passing; mockery murmurs.
O marriage: Hell!
Woman: the devil!
Let boobies trust their wives!

I would entrust
my beer to a German,
all my victuals
to a gluttonous Dutchman,
my flask of aqua vitae to a Turk,

but not my wife to herself. O filthy luck!
That ugly word comes back to my heart:
Horns! Ox! Billy-goat! Twisted antlers!
Ah! Horns! Horns!
But you won't get away from me! Swine, criminal,
damned epicure!
First I'll couple them
and then I'll catch them. I'm exploding!
I'll be avenged for the insult!
May jealousy
forever be praised from the bottom of my heart.

Index of Operas and Arias

Names of arias appear in upper and lower case. Titles of operas are in capital letters; they are alphabetized by full title, including opening articles.

A CATALOG OF SELECTED

DOVER BOOKS

IN ALL FIELDS OF INTEREST

A CATALOG OF SELECTED DOVER
BOOKS IN ALL FIELDS OF INTEREST

CONCERNING THE SPIRITUAL IN ART, Wassily Kandinsky. Pioneering work by father of abstract art. Thoughts on color theory, nature of art. Analysis of earlier masters. 12 illustrations. 80pp. of text. 5⅜ × 8½.　　　23411-8 Pa. $3.95

ANIMALS: 1,419 Copyright-Free Illustrations of Mammals, Birds, Fish, Insects, etc., Jim Harter (ed.). Clear wood engravings present, in extremely lifelike poses, over 1,000 species of animals. One of the most extensive pictorial sourcebooks of its kind. Captions. Index. 284pp. 9 × 12.　　　23766-4 Pa. $12.95

CELTIC ART: The Methods of Construction, George Bain. Simple geometric techniques for making Celtic interlacements, spirals, Kells-type initials, animals, humans, etc. Over 500 illustrations. 160pp. 9 × 12. (USO)　　　22923-8 Pa. $9.95

AN ATLAS OF ANATOMY FOR ARTISTS, Fritz Schider. Most thorough reference work on art anatomy in the world. Hundreds of illustrations, including selections from works by Vesalius, Leonardo, Goya, Ingres, Michelangelo, others. 593 illustrations. 192pp. 7⅞ × 10¼.　　　20241-0 Pa. $9.95

CELTIC HAND STROKE-BY-STROKE (Irish Half-Uncial from "The Book of Kells"): An Arthur Baker Calligraphy Manual, Arthur Baker. Complete guide to creating each letter of the alphabet in distinctive Celtic manner. Covers hand position, strokes, pens, inks, paper, more. Illustrated. 48pp. 8¼ × 11.
24336-2 Pa. $3.95

EASY ORIGAMI, John Montroll. Charming collection of 32 projects (hat, cup, pelican, piano, swan, many more) specially designed for the novice origami hobbyist. Clearly illustrated easy-to-follow instructions insure that even beginning papercrafters will achieve successful results. 48pp. 8¼ × 11.　　　27298-2 Pa. $2.95

THE COMPLETE BOOK OF BIRDHOUSE CONSTRUCTION FOR WOOD-WORKERS, Scott D. Campbell. Detailed instructions, illustrations, tables. Also data on bird habitat and instinct patterns. Bibliography. 3 tables. 63 illustrations in 15 figures. 48pp. 5¼ × 8½.　　　24407-5 Pa. $1.95

BLOOMINGDALE'S ILLUSTRATED 1886 CATALOG: Fashions, Dry Goods and Housewares, Bloomingdale Brothers. Famed merchants' extremely rare catalog depicting about 1,700 products: clothing, housewares, firearms, dry goods, jewelry, more. Invaluable for dating, identifying vintage items. Also, copyright-free graphics for artists, designers. Co-published with Henry Ford Museum & Green-field Village. 160pp. 8¼ × 11.　　　25780-0 Pa. $9.95

HISTORIC COSTUME IN PICTURES, Braun & Schneider. Over 1,450 costumed figures in clearly detailed engravings—from dawn of civilization to end of 19th century. Captions. Many folk costumes. 256pp. 8⅜ × 11¾.　　　23150-X Pa. $11.95

STICKLEY CRAFTSMAN FURNITURE CATALOGS, Gustav Stickley and L. & J. G. Stickley. Beautiful, functional furniture in two authentic catalogs from 1910. 594 illustrations, including 277 photos, show settles, rockers, armchairs, reclining chairs, bookcases, desks, tables. 183pp. 6½ × 9¼. 23838-5 Pa. $9.95

AMERICAN LOCOMOTIVES IN HISTORIC PHOTOGRAPHS: 1858 to 1949, Ron Ziel (ed.). A rare collection of 126 meticulously detailed official photographs, called "builder portraits," of American locomotives that majestically chronicle the rise of steam locomotive power in America. Introduction. Detailed captions. xi + 129pp. 9 × 12. 27393-8 Pa. $12.95

AMERICA'S LIGHTHOUSES: An Illustrated History, Francis Ross Holland, Jr. Delightfully written, profusely illustrated fact-filled survey of over 200 American lighthouses since 1716. History, anecdotes, technological advances, more. 240pp. 8 × 10¾. 25576-X Pa. $11.95

TOWARDS A NEW ARCHITECTURE, Le Corbusier. Pioneering manifesto by founder of "International School." Technical and aesthetic theories, views of industry, economics, relation of form to function, "mass-production split" and much more. Profusely illustrated. 320pp. 6⅛ × 9¼. (USO) 25023-7 Pa. $9.95

HOW THE OTHER HALF LIVES, Jacob Riis. Famous journalistic record, exposing poverty and degradation of New York slums around 1900, by major social reformer. 100 striking and influential photographs. 233pp. 10 × 7⅞. 22012-5 Pa $10.95

FRUIT KEY AND TWIG KEY TO TREES AND SHRUBS, William M. Harlow. One of the handiest and most widely used identification aids. Fruit key covers 120 deciduous and evergreen species; twig key 160 deciduous species. Easily used. Over 300 photographs. 126pp. 5⅜ × 8½. 20511-8 Pa. $3.95

COMMON BIRD SONGS, Dr. Donald J. Borror. Songs of 60 most common U.S. birds: robins, sparrows, cardinals, bluejays, finches, more—arranged in order of increasing complexity. Up to 9 variations of songs of each species. Cassette and manual 99911-4 $8.95

ORCHIDS AS HOUSE PLANTS, Rebecca Tyson Northen. Grow cattleyas and many other kinds of orchids—in a window, in a case, or under artificial light. 63 illustrations. 148pp. 5⅜ × 8½. 23261-1 Pa. $4.95

MONSTER MAZES, Dave Phillips. Masterful mazes at four levels of difficulty. Avoid deadly perils and evil creatures to find magical treasures. Solutions for all 32 exciting illustrated puzzles. 48pp. 8¼ × 11. 26005-4 Pa. $2.95

MOZART'S DON GIOVANNI (DOVER OPERA LIBRETTO SERIES), Wolfgang Amadeus Mozart. Introduced and translated by Ellen H. Bleiler. Standard Italian libretto, with complete English translation. Convenient and thoroughly portable—an ideal companion for reading along with a recording or the performance itself. Introduction. List of characters. Plot summary. 121pp. 5¼ × 8½. 24944-1 Pa. $2.95

TECHNICAL MANUAL AND DICTIONARY OF CLASSICAL BALLET, Gail Grant. Defines, explains, comments on steps, movements, poses and concepts. 15-page pictorial section. Basic book for student, viewer. 127pp. 5⅜ × 8½. 21843-0 Pa. $4.95

BRASS INSTRUMENTS: Their History and Development, Anthony Baines. Authoritative, updated survey of the evolution of trumpets, trombones, bugles, cornets, French horns, tubas and other brass wind instruments. Over 140 illustrations and 48 music examples. Corrected and updated by author. New preface. Bibliography. 320pp. 5⅜ × 8½.   27574-4 Pa. $9.95

HOLLYWOOD GLAMOR PORTRAITS, John Kobal (ed.). 145 photos from 1926–49. Harlow, Gable, Bogart, Bacall; 94 stars in all. Full background on photographers, technical aspects. 160pp. 8⅜ × 11¼.   23352-9 Pa. $11.95

MAX AND MORITZ, Wilhelm Busch. Great humor classic in both German and English. Also 10 other works: "Cat and Mouse," "Plisch and Plumm," etc. 216pp. 5⅜ × 8½.   20181-3 Pa. $5.95

THE RAVEN AND OTHER FAVORITE POEMS, Edgar Allan Poe. Over 40 of the author's most memorable poems: "The Bells," "Ulalume," "Israfel," "To Helen," "The Conqueror Worm," "Eldorado," "Annabel Lee," many more. Alphabetic lists of titles and first lines. 64pp. 5³⁄₁₆ × 8¼.   26685-0 Pa. $1.00

SEVEN SCIENCE FICTION NOVELS, H. G. Wells. The standard collection of the great novels. Complete, unabridged. First Men in the Moon, Island of Dr. Moreau, War of the Worlds, Food of the Gods, Invisible Man, Time Machine, In the Days of the Comet. Total of 1,015pp. 5⅜ × 8½. (USO)   20264-X Clothbd. $29.95

AMULETS AND SUPERSTITIONS, E. A. Wallis Budge. Comprehensive discourse on origin, powers of amulets in many ancient cultures: Arab, Persian, Babylonian, Assyrian, Egyptian, Gnostic, Hebrew, Phoenician, Syriac, etc. Covers cross, swastika, crucifix, seals, rings, stones, etc. 584pp. 5⅜ × 8½. 23573-4 Pa. $12.95

RUSSIAN STORIES/PYCCKNE PACCKA3bl: A Dual-Language Book, edited by Gleb Struve. Twelve tales by such masters as Chekhov, Tolstoy, Dostoevsky, Pushkin, others. Excellent word-for-word English translations on facing pages, plus teaching and study aids, Russian/English vocabulary, biographical/critical introductions, more. 416pp. 5⅜ × 8½.   26244-8 Pa. $8.95

PHILADELPHIA THEN AND NOW: 60 Sites Photographed in the Past and Present, Kenneth Finkel and Susan Oyama. Rare photographs of City Hall, Logan Square, Independence Hall, Betsy Ross House, other landmarks juxtaposed with contemporary views. Captures changing face of historic city. Introduction. Captions. 128pp. 8¼ × 11.   25790-8 Pa. $9.95

AIA ARCHITECTURAL GUIDE TO NASSAU AND SUFFOLK COUNTIES, LONG ISLAND, The American Institute of Architects, Long Island Chapter, and the Society for the Preservation of Long Island Antiquities. Comprehensive, well-researched and generously illustrated volume brings to life over three centuries of Long Island's great architectural heritage. More than 240 photographs with authoritative, extensively detailed captions. 176pp. 8¼ × 11.   26946-9 Pa. $14.95

NORTH AMERICAN INDIAN LIFE: Customs and Traditions of 23 Tribes, Elsie Clews Parsons (ed.). 27 fictionalized essays by noted anthropologists examine religion, customs, government, additional facets of life among the Winnebago, Crow, Zuni, Eskimo, other tribes. 480pp. 6⅛ × 9¼.   27377-6 Pa. $10.95

FRANK LLOYD WRIGHT'S HOLLYHOCK HOUSE, Donald Hoffmann. Lavishly illustrated, carefully documented study of one of Wright's most controversial residential designs. Over 120 photographs, floor plans, elevations, etc. Detailed perceptive text by noted Wright scholar. Index. 128pp. 9¼ × 10¾.
27133-1 Pa. $11.95

THE MALE AND FEMALE FIGURE IN MOTION: 60 Classic Photographic Sequences, Eadweard Muybridge. 60 true-action photographs of men and women walking, running, climbing, bending, turning, etc., reproduced from rare 19th-century masterpiece. vi + 121pp. 9 × 12. 24745-7 Pa. $10.95

1001 QUESTIONS ANSWERED ABOUT THE SEASHORE, N. J. Berrill and Jacquelyn Berrill. Queries answered about dolphins, sea snails, sponges, starfish, fishes, shore birds, many others. Covers appearance, breeding, growth, feeding, much more. 305pp. 5¼ × 8¼. 23366-9 Pa. $7.95

GUIDE TO OWL WATCHING IN NORTH AMERICA, Donald S. Heintzelman. Superb guide offers complete data and descriptions of 19 species: barn owl, screech owl, snowy owl, many more. Expert coverage of owl-watching equipment, conservation, migrations and invasions, etc. Guide to observing sites. 84 illustrations. xiii + 193pp. 5⅜ × 8½. 27344-X Pa. $8.95

MEDICINAL AND OTHER USES OF NORTH AMERICAN PLANTS: A Historical Survey with Special Reference to the Eastern Indian Tribes, Charlotte Erichsen-Brown. Chronological historical citations document 500 years of usage of plants, trees, shrubs native to eastern Canada, northeastern U.S. Also complete identifying information. 343 illustrations. 544pp. 6½ × 9¼. 25951-X Pa. $12.95

STORYBOOK MAZES, Dave Phillips. 23 stories and mazes on two-page spreads: Wizard of Oz, Treasure Island, Robin Hood, etc. Solutions. 64pp. 8¼ × 11.
23628-5 Pa. $2.95

NEGRO FOLK MUSIC, U.S.A., Harold Courlander. Noted folklorist's scholarly yet readable analysis of rich and varied musical tradition. Includes authentic versions of over 40 folk songs. Valuable bibliography and discography. xi + 324pp. 5⅜ × 8½. 27350-4 Pa. $7.95

MOVIE-STAR PORTRAITS OF THE FORTIES, John Kobal (ed.). 163 glamor, studio photos of 106 stars of the 1940s: Rita Hayworth, Ava Gardner, Marlon Brando, Clark Gable, many more. 176pp. 8⅜ × 11¼. 23546-7 Pa. $11.95

BENCHLEY LOST AND FOUND, Robert Benchley. Finest humor from early 30s, about pet peeves, child psychologists, post office and others. Mostly unavailable elsewhere. 73 illustrations by Peter Arno and others. 183pp. 5⅜ × 8½.
22410-4 Pa. $5.95

YEKL and THE IMPORTED BRIDEGROOM AND OTHER STORIES OF YIDDISH NEW YORK, Abraham Cahan. Film Hester Street based on Yekl (1896). Novel, other stories among first about Jewish immigrants on N.Y.'s East Side. 240pp. 5⅜ × 8½. 22427-9 Pa. $6.95

SELECTED POEMS, Walt Whitman. Generous sampling from *Leaves of Grass*. Twenty-four poems include "I Hear America Singing," "Song of the Open Road," "I Sing the Body Electric," "When Lilacs Last in the Dooryard Bloom'd," "O Captain! My Captain!"—all reprinted from an authoritative edition. Lists of titles and first lines. 128pp. 5³⁄₁₆ × 8¼. 26878-0 Pa. $1.00

THE BEST TALES OF HOFFMANN, E. T. A. Hoffmann. 10 of Hoffmann's most important stories: "Nutcracker and the King of Mice," "The Golden Flowerpot," etc. 458pp. 5⅜ × 8½. 21793-0 Pa. $8.95

FROM FETISH TO GOD IN ANCIENT EGYPT, E. A. Wallis Budge. Rich detailed survey of Egyptian conception of "God" and gods, magic, cult of animals, Osiris, more. Also, superb English translations of hymns and legends. 240 illustrations. 545pp. 5⅜ × 8½. 25803-3 Pa. $11.95

FRENCH STORIES/CONTES FRANÇAIS: A Dual-Language Book, Wallace Fowlie. Ten stories by French masters, Voltaire to Camus: "Micromegas" by Voltaire; "The Atheist's Mass" by Balzac; "Minuet" by de Maupassant; "The Guest" by Camus, six more. Excellent English translations on facing pages. Also French-English vocabulary list, exercises, more. 352pp. 5⅜ × 8½. 26443-2 Pa. $8.95

CHICAGO AT THE TURN OF THE CENTURY IN PHOTOGRAPHS: 122 Historic Views from the Collections of the Chicago Historical Society, Larry A. Viskochil. Rare large-format prints offer detailed views of City Hall, State Street, the Loop, Hull House, Union Station, many other landmarks, circa 1904–1913. Introduction. Captions. Maps. 144pp. 9⅜ × 12¼. 24656-6 Pa. $12.95

OLD BROOKLYN IN EARLY PHOTOGRAPHS, 1865–1929, William Lee Younger. Luna Park, Gravesend race track, construction of Grand Army Plaza, moving of Hotel Brighton, etc. 157 previously unpublished photographs. 165pp. 8⅞ × 11¾. 23587-4 Pa. $13.95

THE MYTHS OF THE NORTH AMERICAN INDIANS, Lewis Spence. Rich anthology of the myths and legends of the Algonquins, Iroquois, Pawnees and Sioux, prefaced by an extensive historical and ethnological commentary. 36 illustrations. 480pp. 5⅜ × 8½. 25967-6 Pa. $8.95

AN ENCYCLOPEDIA OF BATTLES: Accounts of Over 1,560 Battles from 1479 B.C. to the Present, David Eggenberger. Essential details of every major battle in recorded history from the first battle of Megiddo in 1479 B.C. to Grenada in 1984. List of Battle Maps. New Appendix covering the years 1967–1984. Index. 99 illustrations. 544pp. 6½ × 9¼. 24913-1 Pa. $14.95

SAILING ALONE AROUND THE WORLD, Captain Joshua Slocum. First man to sail around the world, alone, in small boat. One of great feats of seamanship told in delightful manner. 67 illustrations. 294pp. 5⅜ × 8½. 20326-3 Pa. $5.95

ANARCHISM AND OTHER ESSAYS, Emma Goldman. Powerful, penetrating, prophetic essays on direct action, role of minorities, prison reform, puritan hypocrisy, violence, etc. 271pp. 5⅜ × 8½. 22484-8 Pa. $5.95

MYTHS OF THE HINDUS AND BUDDHISTS, Ananda K. Coomaraswamy and Sister Nivedita. Great stories of the epics; deeds of Krishna, Shiva, taken from puranas, Vedas, folk tales; etc. 32 illustrations. 400pp. 5⅜ × 8½. 21759-0 Pa. $9.95

BEYOND PSYCHOLOGY, Otto Rank. Fear of death, desire of immortality, nature of sexuality, social organization, creativity, according to Rankian system. 291pp. 5⅜ × 8½. 20485-5 Pa. $8.95

A THEOLOGICO-POLITICAL TREATISE, Benedict Spinoza. Also contains unfinished Political Treatise. Great classic on religious liberty, theory of government on common consent. R. Elwes translation. Total of 421pp. 5⅜ × 8½. 20249-6 Pa. $8.95

MY BONDAGE AND MY FREEDOM, Frederick Douglass. Born a slave, Douglass became outspoken force in antislavery movement. The best of Douglass' autobiographies. Graphic description of slave life. 464pp. 5⅜ × 8½.   22457-0 Pa. $8.95

FOLLOWING THE EQUATOR: A Journey Around the World, Mark Twain. Fascinating humorous account of 1897 voyage to Hawaii, Australia, India, New Zealand, etc. Ironic, bemused reports on peoples, customs, climate, flora and fauna, politics, much more. 197 illustrations. 720pp. 5⅜ × 8½.   26113-1 Pa. $15.95

THE PEOPLE CALLED SHAKERS, Edward D. Andrews. Definitive study of Shakers: origins, beliefs, practices, dances, social organization, furniture and crafts, etc. 33 illustrations. 351pp. 5⅜ × 8½.   21081-2 Pa. $8.95

THE MYTHS OF GREECE AND ROME, H. A. Guerber. A classic of mythology, generously illustrated, long prized for its simple, graphic, accurate retelling of the principal myths of Greece and Rome, and for its commentary on their origins and significance. With 64 illustrations by Michelangelo, Raphael, Titian, Rubens, Canova, Bernini and others. 480pp. 5⅜ × 8½.   27584-1 Pa. $9.95

PSYCHOLOGY OF MUSIC, Carl E. Seashore. Classic work discusses music as a medium from psychological viewpoint. Clear treatment of physical acoustics, auditory apparatus, sound perception, development of musical skills, nature of musical feeling, host of other topics. 88 figures. 408pp. 5⅜ × 8½. 21851-1 Pa. $9.95

THE PHILOSOPHY OF HISTORY, Georg W. Hegel. Great classic of Western thought develops concept that history is not chance but rational process, the evolution of freedom. 457pp. 5⅜ × 8½.   20112-0 Pa. $9.95

THE BOOK OF TEA, Kakuzo Okakura. Minor classic of the Orient: entertaining, charming explanation, interpretation of traditional Japanese culture in terms of tea ceremony. 94pp. 5⅜ × 8½.   20070-1 Pa. $3.95

LIFE IN ANCIENT EGYPT, Adolf Erman. Fullest, most thorough, detailed older account with much not in more recent books, domestic life, religion, magic, medicine, commerce, much more. Many illustrations reproduce tomb paintings, carvings, hieroglyphs, etc. 597pp. 5⅜ × 8½.   22632-8 Pa. $10.95

SUNDIALS, Their Theory and Construction, Albert Waugh. Far and away the best, most thorough coverage of ideas, mathematics concerned, types, construction, adjusting anywhere. Simple, nontechnical treatment allows even children to build several of these dials. Over 100 illustrations. 230pp. 5⅜ × 8½.   22947-5 Pa. $7.95

DYNAMICS OF FLUIDS IN POROUS MEDIA, Jacob Bear. For advanced students of ground water hydrology, soil mechanics and physics, drainage and irrigation engineering, and more. 335 illustrations. Exercises, with answers. 784pp. 6⅛ × 9¼.   65675-6 Pa. $19.95

SONGS OF EXPERIENCE: Facsimile Reproduction with 26 Plates in Full Color, William Blake. 26 full-color plates from a rare 1826 edition. Includes "The Tyger," "London," "Holy Thursday," and other poems. Printed text of poems. 48pp. 5¼ × 7.   24636-1 Pa. $4.95

OLD-TIME VIGNETTES IN FULL COLOR, Carol Belanger Grafton (ed.). Over 390 charming, often sentimental illustrations, selected from archives of Victorian graphics—pretty women posing, children playing, food, flowers, kittens and puppies, smiling cherubs, birds and butterflies, much more. All copyright-free. 48pp. 9¼ × 12¼.   27269-9 Pa. $5.95

PERSPECTIVE FOR ARTISTS, Rex Vicat Cole. Depth, perspective of sky and sea, shadows, much more, not usually covered. 391 diagrams, 81 reproductions of drawings and paintings. 279pp. 5⅜ × 8½. 22487-2 Pa. $6.95

DRAWING THE LIVING FIGURE, Joseph Sheppard. Innovative approach to artistic anatomy focuses on specifics of surface anatomy, rather than muscles and bones. Over 170 drawings of live models in front, back and side views, and in widely varying poses. Accompanying diagrams. 177 illustrations. Introduction. Index. 144pp. 8⅜ × 11¼. 26723-7 Pa. $8.95

GOTHIC AND OLD ENGLISH ALPHABETS: 100 Complete Fonts, Dan X. Solo. Add power, elegance to posters, signs, other graphics with 100 stunning copyright-free alphabets: Blackstone, Dolbey, Germania, 97 more—including many lower-case, numerals, punctuation marks. 104pp. 8⅛ × 11. 24695-7 Pa. $8.95

HOW TO DO BEADWORK, Mary White. Fundamental book on craft from simple projects to five-bead chains and woven works. 106 illustrations. 142pp. 5⅜ × 8. 20697-1 Pa. $4.95

THE BOOK OF WOOD CARVING, Charles Marshall Sayers. Finest book for beginners discusses fundamentals and offers 34 designs. "Absolutely first rate . . . well thought out and well executed."—E. J. Tangerman. 118pp. 7¾ × 10⅝. 23654-4 Pa. $5.95

ILLUSTRATED CATALOG OF CIVIL WAR MILITARY GOODS: Union Army Weapons, Insignia, Uniform Accessories, and Other Equipment, Schuyler, Hartley, and Graham. Rare, profusely illustrated 1846 catalog includes Union Army uniform and dress regulations, arms and ammunition, coats, insignia, flags, swords, rifles, etc. 226 illustrations. 160pp. 9 × 12. 24939-5 Pa. $10.95

WOMEN'S FASHIONS OF THE EARLY 1900s: An Unabridged Republication of "New York Fashions, 1909," National Cloak & Suit Co. Rare catalog of mail-order fashions documents women's and children's clothing styles shortly after the turn of the century. Captions offer full descriptions, prices. Invaluable resource for fashion, costume historians. Approximately 725 illustrations. 128pp. 8⅜ × 11¼. 27276-1 Pa. $11.95

THE 1912 AND 1915 GUSTAV STICKLEY FURNITURE CATALOGS, Gustav Stickley. With over 200 detailed illustrations and descriptions, these two catalogs are essential reading and reference materials and identification guides for Stickley furniture. Captions cite materials, dimensions and prices. 112pp. 6½ × 9¼. 26676-1 Pa. $9.95

EARLY AMERICAN LOCOMOTIVES, John H. White, Jr. Finest locomotive engravings from early 19th century: historical (1804–74), main-line (after 1870), special, foreign, etc. 147 plates. 142pp. 11⅜ × 8¼. 22772-3 Pa. $10.95

THE TALL SHIPS OF TODAY IN PHOTOGRAPHS, Frank O. Braynard. Lavishly illustrated tribute to nearly 100 majestic contemporary sailing vessels: Amerigo Vespucci, Clearwater, Constitution, Eagle, Mayflower, Sea Cloud, Victory, many more. Authoritative captions provide statistics, background on each ship. 190 black-and-white photographs and illustrations. Introduction. 128pp. 8⅞ × 11¾. 27163-3 Pa. $13.95

EARLY NINETEENTH-CENTURY CRAFTS AND TRADES, Peter Stockham (ed.). Extremely rare 1807 volume describes to youngsters the crafts and trades of the day: brickmaker, weaver, dressmaker, bookbinder, ropemaker, saddler, many more. Quaint prose, charming illustrations for each craft. 20 black-and-white line illustrations. 192pp. 4⅝ × 6.   27293-1 Pa. $4.95

VICTORIAN FASHIONS AND COSTUMES FROM HARPER'S BAZAR, 1867–1898, Stella Blum (ed.). Day costumes, evening wear, sports clothes, shoes, hats, other accessories in over 1,000 detailed engravings. 320pp. 9⅜ × 12¼.
22990-4 Pa. $13.95

GUSTAV STICKLEY, THE CRAFTSMAN, Mary Ann Smith. Superb study surveys broad scope of Stickley's achievement, especially in architecture. Design philosophy, rise and fall of the Craftsman empire, descriptions and floor plans for many Craftsman houses, more. 86 black-and-white halftones. 31 line illustrations. Introduction. 208pp. 6½ × 9¼.   27210-9 Pa. $9.95

THE LONG ISLAND RAIL ROAD IN EARLY PHOTOGRAPHS, Ron Ziel. Over 220 rare photos, informative text document origin (1844) and development of rail service on Long Island. Vintage views of early trains, locomotives, stations, passengers, crews, much more. Captions. 8⅞ × 11¾.   26301-0 Pa. $13.95

THE BOOK OF OLD SHIPS: From Egyptian Galleys to Clipper Ships, Henry B. Culver. Superb, authoritative history of sailing vessels, with 80 magnificent line illustrations. Galley, bark, caravel, longship, whaler, many more. Detailed, informative text on each vessel by noted naval historian. Introduction. 256pp. 5⅜ × 8½.   27332-6 Pa. $6.95

TEN BOOKS ON ARCHITECTURE, Vitruvius. The most important book ever written on architecture. Early Roman aesthetics, technology, classical orders, site selection, all other aspects. Morgan translation. 331pp. 5⅜ × 8½. 20645-9 Pa. $8.95

THE HUMAN FIGURE IN MOTION, Eadweard Muybridge. More than 4,500 stopped-action photos, in action series, showing undraped men, women, children jumping, lying down, throwing, sitting, wrestling, carrying, etc. 390pp. 7⅞ × 10⅝.
20204-6 Clothbd. $24.95

TREES OF THE EASTERN AND CENTRAL UNITED STATES AND CANADA, William M. Harlow. Best one-volume guide to 140 trees. Full descriptions, woodlore, range, etc. Over 600 illustrations. Handy size. 288pp. 4½ × 6⅜.
20395-6 Pa. $5.95

SONGS OF WESTERN BIRDS, Dr. Donald J. Borror. Complete song and call repertoire of 60 western species, including flycatchers, juncoes, cactus wrens, many more—includes fully illustrated booklet.   Cassette and manual 99913-0 $8.95

GROWING AND USING HERBS AND SPICES, Milo Miloradovich. Versatile handbook provides all the information needed for cultivation and use of all the herbs and spices available in North America. 4 illustrations. Index. Glossary. 236pp. 5⅜ × 8½.   25058-X Pa. $6.95

BIG BOOK OF MAZES AND LABYRINTHS, Walter Shepherd. 50 mazes and labyrinths in all—classical, solid, ripple, and more—in one great volume. Perfect inexpensive puzzler for clever youngsters. Full solutions. 112pp. 8⅛ × 11.
22951-3 Pa. $4.95

PIANO TUNING, J. Cree Fischer. Clearest, best book for beginner, amateur. Simple repairs, raising dropped notes, tuning by easy method of flattened fifths. No previous skills needed. 4 illustrations. 201pp. 5⅜ × 8½.   23267-0 Pa. $5.95

A SOURCE BOOK IN THEATRICAL HISTORY, A. M. Nagler. Contemporary observers on acting, directing, make-up, costuming, stage props, machinery, scene design, from Ancient Greece to Chekhov. 611pp. 5⅜ × 8½.   20515-0 Pa. $11.95

THE COMPLETE NONSENSE OF EDWARD LEAR, Edward Lear. All nonsense limericks, zany alphabets, Owl and Pussycat, songs, nonsense botany, etc., illustrated by Lear. Total of 320pp. 5⅜ × 8½. (USO)   20167-8 Pa. $6.95

VICTORIAN PARLOUR POETRY: An Annotated Anthology, Michael R. Turner. 117 gems by Longfellow, Tennyson, Browning, many lesser-known poets. "The Village Blacksmith," "Curfew Must Not Ring Tonight," "Only a Baby Small," dozens more, often difficult to find elsewhere. Index of poets, titles, first lines. xxiii + 325pp. 5⅜ × 8¼.   27044-0 Pa. $8.95

DUBLINERS, James Joyce. Fifteen stories offer vivid, tightly focused observations of the lives of Dublin's poorer classes. At least one, "The Dead," is considered a masterpiece. Reprinted complete and unabridged from standard edition. 160pp. 5³⁄₁₆ × 8¼.   26870-5 Pa. $1.00

THE HAUNTED MONASTERY and THE CHINESE MAZE MURDERS, Robert van Gulik. Two full novels by van Gulik, set in 7th-century China, continue adventures of Judge Dee and his companions. An evil Taoist monastery, seemingly supernatural events; overgrown topiary maze hides strange crimes. 27 illustrations. 328pp. 5⅜ × 8½.   23502-5 Pa. $7.95

THE BOOK OF THE SACRED MAGIC OF ABRAMELIN THE MAGE, translated by S. MacGregor Mathers. Medieval manuscript of ceremonial magic. Basic document in Aleister Crowley, Golden Dawn groups. 268pp. 5⅜ × 8½.
          23211-5 Pa. $8.95

NEW RUSSIAN-ENGLISH AND ENGLISH-RUSSIAN DICTIONARY, M. A. O'Brien. This is a remarkably handy Russian dictionary, containing a surprising amount of information, including over 70,000 entries. 366pp. 4½ × 6⅛.
          20208-9 Pa. $9.95

HISTORIC HOMES OF THE AMERICAN PRESIDENTS, Second, Revised Edition, Irvin Haas. A traveler's guide to American Presidential homes, most open to the public, depicting and describing homes occupied by every American President from George Washington to George Bush. With visiting hours, admission charges, travel routes. 175 photographs. Index. 160pp. 8¼ × 11. 26751-2 Pa. $10.95

NEW YORK IN THE FORTIES, Andreas Feininger. 162 brilliant photographs by the well-known photographer, formerly with *Life* magazine. Commuters, shoppers, Times Square at night, much else from city at its peak. Captions by John von Hartz. 181pp. 9¼ × 10¾.   23585-8 Pa. $12.95

INDIAN SIGN LANGUAGE, William Tomkins. Over 525 signs developed by Sioux and other tribes. Written instructions and diagrams. Also 290 pictographs. 111pp. 6⅛ × 9¼.   22029-X Pa. $3.50

ANATOMY: A Complete Guide for Artists, Joseph Sheppard. A master of figure drawing shows artists how to render human anatomy convincingly. Over 460 illustrations. 224pp. 8⅜ × 11¼. 27279-6 Pa. $10.95

MEDIEVAL CALLIGRAPHY: Its History and Technique, Marc Drogin. Spirited history, comprehensive instruction manual covers 13 styles (ca. 4th century thru 15th). Excellent photographs; directions for duplicating medieval techniques with modern tools. 224pp. 8⅜ × 11¼. 26142-5 Pa. $11.95

DRIED FLOWERS: How to Prepare Them, Sarah Whitlock and Martha Rankin. Complete instructions on how to use silica gel, meal and borax, perlite aggregate, sand and borax, glycerine and water to create attractive permanent flower arrangements. 12 illustrations. 32pp. 5⅜ × 8½. 21802-3 Pa. $1.00

EASY-TO-MAKE BIRD FEEDERS FOR WOODWORKERS, Scott D. Campbell. Detailed, simple-to-use guide for designing, constructing, caring for and using feeders. Text, illustrations for 12 classic and contemporary designs. 96pp. 5⅜ × 8½. 25847-5 Pa. $2.95

OLD-TIME CRAFTS AND TRADES, Peter Stockham. An 1807 book created to teach children about crafts and trades open to them as future careers. It describes in detailed, nontechnical terms 24 different occupations, among them coachmaker, gardener, hairdresser, lacemaker, shoemaker, wheelwright, copper-plate printer, milliner, trunkmaker, merchant and brewer. Finely detailed engravings illustrate each occupation. 192pp. 4⅝ × 6. 27398-9 Pa. $4.95

THE HISTORY OF UNDERCLOTHES, C. Willett Cunnington and Phyllis Cunnington. Fascinating, well-documented survey covering six centuries of English undergarments, enhanced with over 100 illustrations: 12th-century laced-up bodice, footed long drawers (1795), 19th-century bustles, 19th-century corsets for men, Victorian "bust improvers," much more. 272pp. 5⅜ × 8¼. 27124-2 Pa. $9.95

ARTS AND CRAFTS FURNITURE: The Complete Brooks Catalog of 1912, Brooks Manufacturing Co. Photos and detailed descriptions of more than 150 now very collectible furniture designs from the Arts and Crafts movement depict davenports, settees, buffets, desks, tables, chairs, bedsteads, dressers and more, all built of solid, quarter-sawed oak. Invaluable for students and enthusiasts of antiques, Americana and the decorative arts. 80pp. 6½ × 9¼. 27471-3 Pa. $7.95

HOW WE INVENTED THE AIRPLANE: An Illustrated History, Orville Wright. Fascinating firsthand account covers early experiments, construction of planes and motors, first flights, much more. Introduction and commentary by Fred C. Kelly. 76 photographs. 96pp. 8¼ × 11. 25662-6 Pa. $8.95

THE ARTS OF THE SAILOR: Knotting, Splicing and Ropework, Hervey Garrett Smith. Indispensable shipboard reference covers tools, basic knots and useful hitches; handsewing and canvas work, more. Over 100 illustrations. Delightful reading for sea lovers. 256pp. 5⅜ × 8½. 26440-8 Pa. $7.95

FRANK LLOYD WRIGHT'S FALLINGWATER: The House and Its History, Second, Revised Edition, Donald Hoffmann. A total revision—both in text and illustrations—of the standard document on Fallingwater, the boldest, most personal architectural statement of Wright's mature years, updated with valuable new material from the recently opened Frank Lloyd Wright Archives. "Fascinating"—*The New York Times*. 116 illustrations. 128pp. 9¼ × 10¾. 27430-6 Pa. $10.95

CATALOG OF DOVER BOOKS

PHOTOGRAPHIC SKETCHBOOK OF THE CIVIL WAR, Alexander Gardner. 100 photos taken on field during the Civil War. Famous shots of Manassas, Harper's Ferry, Lincoln, Richmond, slave pens, etc. 244pp. 10⅝ × 8¼.
22731-6 Pa. $9.95

FIVE ACRES AND INDEPENDENCE, Maurice G. Kains. Great back-to-the-land classic explains basics of self-sufficient farming. The one book to get. 95 illustrations. 397pp. 5⅜ × 8½. 20974-1 Pa. $7.95

SONGS OF EASTERN BIRDS, Dr. Donald J. Borror. Songs and calls of 60 species most common to eastern U.S.: warblers, woodpeckers, flycatchers, thrushes, larks, many more in high-quality recording. Cassette and manual 99912-2 $8.95

A MODERN HERBAL, Margaret Grieve. Much the fullest, most exact, most useful compilation of herbal material. Gigantic alphabetical encyclopedia, from aconite to zedoary, gives botanical information, medical properties, folklore, economic uses, much else. Indispensable to serious reader. 161 illustrations. 888pp. 6½ × 9¼. 2-vol. set. (USO) Vol. I: 22798-7 Pa. $9.95
Vol. II: 22799-5 Pa. $9.95

HIDDEN TREASURE MAZE BOOK, Dave Phillips. Solve 34 challenging mazes accompanied by heroic tales of adventure. Evil dragons, people-eating plants, bloodthirsty giants, many more dangerous adversaries lurk at every twist and turn. 34 mazes, stories, solutions. 48pp. 8¼ × 11. 24566-7 Pa. $2.95

LETTERS OF W. A. MOZART, Wolfgang A. Mozart. Remarkable letters show bawdy wit, humor, imagination, musical insights, contemporary musical world; includes some letters from Leopold Mozart. 276pp. 5⅜ × 8½. 22859-2 Pa. $7.95

BASIC PRINCIPLES OF CLASSICAL BALLET, Agrippina Vaganova. Great Russian theoretician, teacher explains methods for teaching classical ballet. 118 illustrations. 175pp. 5⅜ × 8½. 22036-2 Pa. $4.95

THE JUMPING FROG, Mark Twain. Revenge edition. The original story of The Celebrated Jumping Frog of Calaveras County, a hapless French translation, and Twain's hilarious "retranslation" from the French. 12 illustrations. 66pp. 5⅜ × 8½.
22686-7 Pa. $3.95

BEST REMEMBERED POEMS, Martin Gardner (ed.). The 126 poems in this superb collection of 19th- and 20th-century British and American verse range from Shelley's "To a Skylark" to the impassioned "Renascence" of Edna St. Vincent Millay and to Edward Lear's whimsical "The Owl and the Pussycat." 224pp. 5⅜ × 8½.
27165-X Pa. $4.95

COMPLETE SONNETS, William Shakespeare. Over 150 exquisite poems deal with love, friendship, the tyranny of time, beauty's evanescence, death and other themes in language of remarkable power, precision and beauty. Glossary of archaic terms. 80pp. 5³⁄₁₆ × 8¼. 26686-9 Pa. $1.00

BODIES IN A BOOKSHOP, R. T. Campbell. Challenging mystery of blackmail and murder with ingenious plot and superbly drawn characters. In the best tradition of British suspense fiction. 192pp. 5⅜ × 8½. 24720-1 Pa. $5.95

THE WIT AND HUMOR OF OSCAR WILDE, Alvin Redman (ed.). More than 1,000 ripostes, paradoxes, wisecracks: Work is the curse of the drinking classes; I can resist everything except temptation; etc. 258pp. 5⅜ × 8½. 20602-5 Pa. $5.95

SHAKESPEARE LEXICON AND QUOTATION DICTIONARY, Alexander Schmidt. Full definitions, locations, shades of meaning in every word in plays and poems. More than 50,000 exact quotations. 1,485pp. 6½ × 9¼. 2-vol. set.
Vol. 1: 22726-X Pa. $16.95
Vol. 2: 22727-8 Pa. $15.95

SELECTED POEMS, Emily Dickinson. Over 100 best-known, best-loved poems by one of America's foremost poets, reprinted from authoritative early editions. No comparable edition at this price. Index of first lines. 64pp. 5³⁄₁₆ × 8¼.
26466-1 Pa. $1.00

CELEBRATED CASES OF JUDGE DEE (DEE GOONG AN), translated by Robert van Gulik. Authentic 18th-century Chinese detective novel; Dee and associates solve three interlocked cases. Led to van Gulik's own stories with same characters. Extensive introduction. 9 illustrations. 237pp. 5⅜ × 8½.
23337-5 Pa. $6.95

THE MALLEUS MALEFICARUM OF KRAMER AND SPRENGER, translated by Montague Summers. Full text of most important witchhunter's "bible," used by both Catholics and Protestants. 278pp. 6⅝ × 10. 22802-9 Pa. $11.95

SPANISH STORIES/CUENTOS ESPAÑOLES: A Dual-Language Book, Angel Flores (ed.). Unique format offers 13 great stories in Spanish by Cervantes, Borges, others. Faithful English translations on facing pages. 352pp. 5⅜ × 8½.
25399-6 Pa. $8.95

THE CHICAGO WORLD'S FAIR OF 1893: A Photographic Record, Stanley Appelbaum (ed.). 128 rare photos show 200 buildings, Beaux-Arts architecture, Midway, original Ferris Wheel, Edison's kinetoscope, more. Architectural emphasis; full text. 116pp. 8¼ × 11. 23990-X Pa. $9.95

OLD QUEENS, N.Y., IN EARLY PHOTOGRAPHS, Vincent F. Seyfried and William Asadorian. Over 160 rare photographs of Maspeth, Jamaica, Jackson Heights, and other areas. Vintage views of DeWitt Clinton mansion, 1939 World's Fair and more. Captions. 192pp. 8⅞ × 11. 26358-4 Pa. $12.95

CAPTURED BY THE INDIANS: 15 Firsthand Accounts, 1750–1870, Frederick Drimmer. Astounding true historical accounts of grisly torture, bloody conflicts, relentless pursuits, miraculous escapes and more, by people who lived to tell the tale. 384pp. 5⅜ × 8½. 24901-8 Pa. $8.95

THE WORLD'S GREAT SPEECHES, Lewis Copeland and Lawrence W. Lamm (eds.). Vast collection of 278 speeches of Greeks to 1970. Powerful and effective models; unique look at history. 842pp. 5⅜ × 8½. 20468-5 Pa. $14.95

THE BOOK OF THE SWORD, Sir Richard F. Burton. Great Victorian scholar/adventurer's eloquent, erudite history of the "queen of weapons"—from prehistory to early Roman Empire. Evolution and development of early swords, variations (sabre, broadsword, cutlass, scimitar, etc.), much more. 336pp. 6⅛ × 9¼. 25434-8 Pa. $8.95

AUTOBIOGRAPHY: The Story of My Experiments with Truth, Mohandas K. Gandhi. Boyhood, legal studies, purification, the growth of the Satyagraha (nonviolent protest) movement. Critical, inspiring work of the man responsible for the freedom of India. 480pp. 5⅜ × 8½. (USO)   24593-4 Pa. $8.95

CELTIC MYTHS AND LEGENDS, T. W. Rolleston. Masterful retelling of Irish and Welsh stories and tales. Cuchulain, King Arthur, Deirdre, the Grail, many more. First paperback edition. 58 full-page illustrations. 512pp. 5⅜ × 8½.
26507-2 Pa. $9.95

THE PRINCIPLES OF PSYCHOLOGY, William James. Famous long course complete, unabridged. Stream of thought, time perception, memory, experimental methods; great work decades ahead of its time. 94 figures. 1,391pp. 5⅜ × 8½. 2-vol. set.
Vol. I: 20381-6 Pa. $12.95
Vol. II: 20382-4 Pa. $12.95

THE WORLD AS WILL AND REPRESENTATION, Arthur Schopenhauer. Definitive English translation of Schopenhauer's life work, correcting more than 1,000 errors, omissions in earlier translations. Translated by E. F. J. Payne. Total of 1,269pp. 5⅜ × 8½. 2-vol. set.   Vol. 1: 21761-2 Pa. $11.95
Vol. 2: 21762-0 Pa. $11.95

MAGIC AND MYSTERY IN TIBET, Madame Alexandra David-Neel. Experiences among lamas, magicians, sages, sorcerers, Bonpa wizards. A true psychic discovery. 32 illustrations. 321pp. 5⅜ × 8½. (USO)   22682-4 Pa. $8.95

THE EGYPTIAN BOOK OF THE DEAD, E. A. Wallis Budge. Complete reproduction of Ani's papyrus, finest ever found. Full hieroglyphic text, interlinear transliteration, word-for-word translation, smooth translation. 533pp. 6½ × 9¼.
21866-X Pa. $9.95

MATHEMATICS FOR THE NONMATHEMATICIAN, Morris Kline. Detailed, college-level treatment of mathematics in cultural and historical context, with numerous exercises. Recommended Reading Lists. Tables. Numerous figures. 641pp. 5⅜ × 8½.   24823-2 Pa. $11.95

THEORY OF WING SECTIONS: Including a Summary of Airfoil Data, Ira H. Abbott and A. E. von Doenhoff. Concise compilation of subsonic aerodynamic characteristics of NACA wing sections, plus description of theory. 350pp. of tables. 693pp. 5⅜ × 8½.   60586-8 Pa. $14.95

THE RIME OF THE ANCIENT MARINER, Gustave Doré, S. T. Coleridge. Doré's finest work; 34 plates capture moods, subtleties of poem. Flawless full-size reproductions printed on facing pages with authoritative text of poem. "Beautiful. Simply beautiful."—*Publisher's Weekly.* 77pp. 9¼ × 12.   22305-1 Pa. $6.95

NORTH AMERICAN INDIAN DESIGNS FOR ARTISTS AND CRAFTS-PEOPLE, Eva Wilson. Over 360 authentic copyright-free designs adapted from Navajo blankets, Hopi pottery, Sioux buffalo hides, more. Geometrics, symbolic figures, plant and animal motifs, etc. 128pp. 8⅜ × 11. (EUK)   25341-4 Pa. $7.95

SCULPTURE: Principles and Practice, Louis Slobodkin. Step-by-step approach to clay, plaster, metals, stone; classical and modern. 253 drawings, photos. 255pp. 8⅛ × 11.   22960-2 Pa. $10.95

THE INFLUENCE OF SEA POWER UPON HISTORY, 1660–1783, A. T. Mahan. Influential classic of naval history and tactics still used as text in war colleges. First paperback edition. 4 maps. 24 battle plans. 640pp. 5⅜ × 8½.

25509-3 Pa. $12.95

THE STORY OF THE TITANIC AS TOLD BY ITS SURVIVORS, Jack Winocour (ed.). What it was really like. Panic, despair, shocking inefficiency, and a little heroism. More thrilling than any fictional account. 26 illustrations. 320pp. 5⅜ × 8½.

20610-6 Pa. $8.95

FAIRY AND FOLK TALES OF THE IRISH PEASANTRY, William Butler Yeats (ed.). Treasury of 64 tales from the twilight world of Celtic myth and legend: "The Soul Cages," "The Kildare Pooka," "King O'Toole and his Goose," many more. Introduction and Notes by W. B. Yeats. 352pp. 5⅜ × 8½.

26941-8 Pa. $8.95

BUDDHIST MAHAYANA TEXTS, E. B. Cowell and Others (eds.). Superb, accurate translations of basic documents in Mahayana Buddhism, highly important in history of religions. The Buddha-karita of Asvaghosha, Larger Sukhavativyuha, more. 448pp. 5⅜ × 8½. ,

25552-2 Pa. $9.95

ONE TWO THREE . . . INFINITY: Facts and Speculations of Science, George Gamow. Great physicist's fascinating, readable overview of contemporary science: number theory, relativity, fourth dimension, entropy, genes, atomic structure, much more. 128 illustrations. Index. 352pp. 5⅜ × 8½.

25664-2 Pa. $8.95

ENGINEERING IN HISTORY, Richard Shelton Kirby, et al. Broad, nontechnical survey of history's major technological advances: birth of Greek science, industrial revolution, electricity and applied science, 20th-century automation, much more. 181 illustrations. ". . . excellent . . ."—Isis. Bibliography. vii + 530pp. 5⅜ × 8¼.

26412-2 Pa. $14.95

Prices subject to change without notice.

Available at your book dealer or write for free catalog to Dept. GI, Dover Publications, Inc., 31 East 2nd St., Mineola, N.Y. 11501. Dover publishes more than 500 books each year on science, elementary and advanced mathematics, biology, music, art, literary history, social sciences and other areas.